Suppers

BLOOMSBURY KITCHEN LIBRARY

Suppers

Bloomsbury Books
London

This edition published 1995 by Bloomsbury Books,
an imprint of The Godfrey Cave Group,
42 Bloomsbury Street, London, WC1B 3QJ.

ISBN 1 85471 513 5

Printed and bound in Great Britain

Contents

Barquettes with Three Fillings

Serves 6		Calories
Working time: about 1 hour		260
		Protein
		12g
Total time: about 2 hours and 15 minutes (includes chilling)		Cholesterol 40mg
		Total fat 15g
		Saturated fat 4g
		Sodium 490mg

125 g	plain flour	4 oz	$\frac{1}{4}$ tsp	salt	$\frac{1}{4}$ tsp
$\frac{1}{8}$ tsp	salt	$\frac{1}{8}$ tsp		freshly ground black pepper	
60 g	polyunsaturated margarine	2 oz	2 tsp	fresh lemon juice	2 tsp
$\frac{1}{2}$	beaten egg	$\frac{1}{2}$	3	thin slices of lemon, quartered	3
	Asparagus cream			**Prawn salad**	
175 g	thin asparagus spears, trimmed	6 oz	1 tsp	virgin olive oil	1 tsp
1 tbsp	soured cream	1 tbsp	1 tsp	wine vinegar	1 tsp
$\frac{1}{8}$ tsp	salt	$\frac{1}{8}$ tsp	1	garlic clove, crushed	1
	freshly ground black pepper		2 tsp	finely chopped parsley	2 tsp
	Smoked mackerel mousse			freshly ground black pepper	
175 g	smoked mackerel fillet, skinned	6 oz	90 g	peeled prawns	3 oz
15 g	polyunsaturated margarine	$\frac{1}{2}$ oz	2	lettuce leaves, shredded	2

Sift the flour and salt into a bowl. Rub the margarine into the flour until the mixture resembles fine breadcrumbs. Mix the dry ingredients together with the beaten egg and 1 to 2 tablespoons of water to make a firm dough.

Roll out the dough and cut it into strips to line eighteen 9.5 cm (3$\frac{3}{4}$ inch) long barquette tins. Prick the dough then refrigerate for 30 minutes. Preheat the oven to 220°C (425°F or Mark 7). Bake the pastry cases until lightly browned.

Flake the fish and put it into a blender with the margarine, salt, pepper and the lemon juice. Blend until smooth, cover, and refrigerate.

Boil the asparagus until tender, drain and refresh. Finely chop the asparagus (leaving six tips for garnish) and mix with the soured cream, salt and pepper. Cover and refrigerate.

Mix the prawns with the oil, vinegar, garlic and parsley, cover and refrigerate. Chill all three fillings for at least 1 hour before serving.

Lasagne Roll-Ups

Serves 6

Working time: about 45 minutes

Total time: about 1 hour and 10 minutes

Calories 445
Protein 24g
Cholesterol 35mg
Total fat 16g
Saturated fat 7g
Sodium 340mg

12	lasagne strips	12	2	small carrots, chopped	2
500 g	ricotta cheese	1 lb	2	sticks celery, chopped	2
125 g	mozzarella, shredded	4 oz	2	garlic cloves, thinly sliced	2
250 g	broccoli, steamed and chopped	8 oz	3 tbsp	chopped fresh basil,	3 tbsp
75 g	mushrooms, sliced	2½ oz		freshly ground black pepper	
2	spring onions, chopped	2	1	bay leaf	1
2 tbsp	chopped fresh basil	2 tbsp	15 cl	Madeira	¼ pint
1 tbsp	chopped fresh oregano	1 tbsp	1.25 kg	ripe tomatoes, skinned,	2½ lb
4 tbsp	chopped parsley	4 tbsp		seeded and chopped	
	Tomato sauce		2 tbsp	tomato paste	2 tbsp
2 tbsp	safflower oil	2 tbsp	125 g	unsweetened apple purée	4 oz
1	onion, coarsely chopped	1	3 tbsp	grated Parmesan cheese	3 tbsp

Gently sauté the onion, carrots and celery over medium-high heat for 2 minutes. Stir in the garlic, basil, pepper, bay leaf and Madeira. Cook until it is reduced by half. Add the tomatoes, tomato paste and apple purée. Return to the boil, then simmer for 30 to 35 minutes. Remove the bay leaf and purée the sauce in a blender. Add the Parmesan and set aside.

Preheat the oven to 180°C (350°F or Mark 4). Cook the lasagne until it is *al dente*, and drain it.

Mix the ricotta, mozzarella, oregano, broccoli, mushrooms, spring onions, basil and parsley.

Spread ¼ litre (8 fl oz) of the tomato sauce in a large baking dish. Spread 4 tablespoons of the cheese and vegetable mixture over a lasagne strip, roll it up and place in the dish. Repeat with the remaining strips and filling. Pour on the rest of the sauce and cover, bake for 20 minutes, then remove the foil and bake for 15 to 20 minutes more. Serve hot.

8

Lasagne Layered with Spinach

Serves 8

Working time:
about 20
minutes

Total time:
about 1 hour
and
15 minutes

Calories
300
Protein
20g
Cholesterol
40mg
Total fat
13g
Saturated fat
8g
Sodium
410mg

8	lasagne strips	**8**
30 g	unsalted butter	**1 oz**
1	medium onion, finely chopped	**1**
2	garlic cloves, finely chopped	**2**
125 g	mushrooms, thinly sliced	**4 oz**
800 g	canned tomatoes, drained and coarsely chopped, the juice reserved	**28 oz**
4 tbsp	tomato paste	**4 tbsp**
4 tbsp	red wine	**4 tbsp**
1 tbsp	chopped fresh oregano	**1 tbsp**
2 tbsp	chopped fresh basil leaves	**2 tbsp**
2 tbsp	dark brown sugar	**2 tbsp**
½ tsp	salt	**½ tsp**
	freshly ground black pepper	
2 tbsp	grated Parmesan cheese	**2 tbsp**
500 g	ricotta cheese	**1 lb**
1	egg white	**1**
500 g	fresh spinach, rinsed, stemmed and blanched for 1 minute	**1 lb**
250 g	mozzarella, thinly sliced	**½ lb**

Put the butter in a 2 litre (3½ pint) glass bowl, cover, and microwave on high until the butter is melted—about 1 minute. Mix in the onion, garlic and mushrooms. Cover and microwave it on medium high for 2 minutes. Add the tomatoes, the reserved juice, the tomato paste, wine, oregano, basil, sugar, salt and some pepper, and stir well. Cover the bowl with a paper towel and microwave the contents on high for 12 minutes, stirring every 4 minutes. Stir in the Parmesan and set aside.

Mix the ricotta with the egg white and some more pepper. Add the spinach and mix well.

Spread 12.5 cl (4 fl oz) of the sauce evenly over the bottom of a shallow dish. Lay uncooked lasagne strips side by side in the sauce, then cover them with a layer of the spinach mixture and a layer of mozzarella slices. Repeat the layering process and top the dish with the remaining sauce. Cover with plastic film, leaving a corner open; microwave it on high for 6 minutes, then on medium high for 20 minutes more. Let stand for 15 minutes before serving.

Spaghetti with Smoked Salmon and Watercress

Serves 2

Working
(and total)
time: about
15 minutes

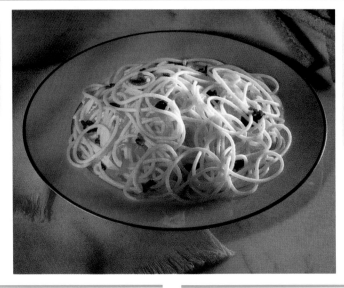

Calories
245
Protein
10g
Cholesterol
5mg
Total fat
3g
Saturated fat
0g
Sodium
215mg

125 g	spaghetti	4 oz	1	bunch watercress, washed	1
1 tsp	virgin olive oil	1 tsp		and stemmed	
½	garlic clove, finely chopped	½		freshly ground black pepper	
30 g	smoked salmon, julienned	1 oz			

Cook the spaghetti in 1 ½ litres (2 ½ pts) of boiling water with ¾ teaspoon of salt. Start testing the pasta after 8 minutes and cook it until it is *al dente*.

Just before the spaghetti finishes cooking, heat the oil in a large frying pan over medium heat. Cook the garlic in the oil for 30 seconds, stirring constantly. Add the salmon, watercress and pepper, and cook for 30 seconds more before removing the pan from the heat.

Drain the spaghetti and add it to the pan. Toss the spaghetti and serve at once.

Spanish-Style Chicken and Saffron Rice

Serves 4

Working time: about 30 minutes

Total time: about 1 hour and 30 minutes

Calories 570

Protein 41g

Cholesterol 105mg

Total fat 20g

Saturated fat 4g

Sodium 410mg

1.25 kg	chicken, skinned, cut into serving pieces	**2½ lb**
	freshly ground black pepper	
½ tsp	salt	**½ tsp**
3 tbsp	virgin olive oil	**3 tbsp**
2	medium onions, thinly sliced	**2**
175 g	long-grain brown rice	**6 oz**
12.5 cl	dry white wine	**4 fl oz**
⅛ tsp	crushed saffron threads	**⅛ tsp**
35 cl	unsalted chicken stock	**12 fl oz**

2 tbsp	mildly hot chillies	**2 tbsp**
⅛ tsp	crushed cumin seeds	**⅛ tsp**
2	garlic cloves, finely chopped	**2**
2	large ripe tomatoes, skinned, seeded and chopped	**2**
1	each red and yellow sweet pepper, grilled, skinned, seeded and cut into 2.5 cm (1 inch) strips	**1**
	fresh coriander for garnish (optional)	

Sprinkle the chicken pieces with pepper and ¼ teaspoon of salt. In a lidded fireproof 4 litre (7 pint) casserole, heat 2 tablespoons of the olive oil over medium-high heat Sauté the chicken until golden-brown—about 4 minutes on each side—and remove to a plate.

Add the remaining tablespoon of oil to the casserole and cook the onions over medium heat until translucent—about 10 minutes. Add the brown rice and cook 2 minutes, stirring constantly to coat the grains thoroughly; pour in the white wine, bring to the boil, then reduce the heat, cover, and simmer until all the liquid has been absorbed—about 8 minutes. Add the saffron to the stock and pour over the rice. Stir in the chillies, cumin seeds, the remaining salt and the garlic. Simmer 15 minutes more and add the tomatoes and chicken, pushing them down into the rice. Cook until the juices run clear when a thigh is pierced with the tip of a sharp knife—about 25 minutes more. Garnish with the pepper strips and coriander

Brown Rice and Mango Salad

Serves 8 as a
side dish

Working time:
about 20
minutes

Total time:
about 1 hour
and 30
minutes

Calories
140
Protein
2g
Cholesterol
0mg
Total fat
4g
Saturated fat
0g
Sodium
70mg

185 g	brown rice	**6½ oz**
4 tbsp	red wine vinegar	**4 tbsp**
¼ tsp	salt	**¼ tsp**
2 tbsp	safflower oil	**2 tbsp**
1	sweet green pepper, seeded and deribbed	**1**
1	small shallot, finely chopped	**1**
⅛ tsp	ground cardamom	**⅛ tsp**
	mace	
	cayenne pepper	
1	ripe mango, peeled and diced	**1**

Bring 1.5 litres (2 ½ pints) of water to the boil in a large saucepan. Stir in the rice, reduce the heat and simmer the rice, uncovered, until it is tender—about 35 minutes. Drain the rice and put it in a serving bowl. Stir in the vinegar and salt, and allow the mixture to cool to room temperature—about 30 minutes.

When the rice is cool, stir in the oil, pepper, shallot, cardamom and a pinch each of mace and cayenne pepper. Add the mango pieces and stir them in gently so that they retain their shape. Cover the salad; to allow the flavours to meld, let the salad stand, unrefrigerated, for about 30 minutes before serving it.

Leek and Bacon Potatoes

Serves 4

Working time: about 15 minutes

Total time: about 25 minutes

Calories 145

Protein 8g

Cholesterol 10mg

Total fat 2g

Saturated fat trace

Sodium 340mg

4	potatoes, scrubbed and pricked all over with a fork	4
60 g	lean smoked bacon, trimmed of fat and diced	2 oz
125 g	leeks, trimmed, cleaned and finely chopped	4 oz
1 tbsp	skimmed milk	1 tbsp
	freshly ground black pepper	

Place the potatoes in a circle on a paper towel in the microwave oven. Cook on high for 10 minutes, turning after 5 minutes, then remove them from the oven and set them aside.

Put the bacon and leeks in a small bowl and microwave on high for 3 minutes, stirring once.

Cut the tops off the potatoes and scoop out the insides to within 5 mm ($\frac{1}{4}$ inch) of the skins. Mash the scooped out potato with the milk and season lightly with freshly ground pepper. Stir in the bacon and leeks. Pile the potato, bacon and leek mixture back into the skins, place the lids on top and reheat on high for 1 to 2 minutes before serving.

Scallop and Lime Choux Puffs

Makes 16
puffs

Working
time: about
40 minutes

Total time:
about 1 hour
and 20
minutes

Per puff:
Calories
80
Protein
6g
Cholesterol
45mg
Total fat
4g
Saturated fat
2g
Sodium
105mg

350 g	raw scallops, bright white connective tissue removed, rinsed and diced	**12 oz**	**¼ tsp**	salt freshly ground black pepper	**¼ tsp**	
1½ tsp	cornflour	**1½ tsp**		**60 g**	fromage frais	**2 oz**
1½ tbsp	fresh lime juice	**1½ tbsp**			**Choux dough**	
¼ tsp	grated lime rind	**¼ tsp**		**60 g**	unsalted butter	**2 oz**
1½ tbsp	finely chopped parsley	**1½ tbsp**		**¼ tsp**	salt	**¼ tsp**
				75 g	plain flour	**2½ oz**

To make the choux dough, place the butter and salt in a small saucepan containing 15 cl (¼ pint) of water, and heat to boiling point. Add all the flour, and beat the mixture until it comes away cleanly from the pan sides. Remove the pan from the heat.

Beat the eggs with a little cayenne pepper, then add them to the dough; beat until the eggs are absorbed and a stiff paste is formed.

Preheat the oven to 230°C (450°F or Mark 8). Lightly oil a baking sheet. Fit a piping bag with a plain nozzle, fill it with choux dough and pipe 16 walnut-sized rounds on to the baking sheet. Cook the choux rounds in the oven for 10 minutes. Lower the heat to 180°C (350°F or Mark 4) and cook for a further 25 to 30 minutes until the puffs are golden.

Slice through each choux puff about a third of the way from the top to allow the steam to escape, and leave to cool until required.

For the filling, coat the scallops with the cornflour and sear them in a dry pan over a medium-high heat until they begin to colour. Reduce the heat, add the lime juice and rind, parsley, salt, some pepper and the fromage frais. Continue to cook until the juices thicken—about 2 minutes.

Warm the choux puffs through in a 180°C (350°F or Mark 4) oven. Spoon the scallop filling into the puffs and serve immediately.

Chick-Pea and Yogurt Dip

Serves 6

Working time:
about 15
minutes

Total time:
about 2 hours
(includes
soaking)

Calories
145

Protein
9g

Cholesterol
2mg

Total fat
3g

Saturated fat
trace

Sodium
160mg

250 g	dried chick-peas	8 oz
2 tbsp	tahini	2 tbsp
12.5 cl	plain low-fat yogurt	4 fl oz
3	garlic cloves, crushed	3
2	lemons, juice only	2

$\frac{1}{2}$ tsp	salt	$\frac{1}{2}$ tsp
	freshly ground black pepper	
	paprika, for garnish	
	chopped parsley, for garnish	

Rinse the chick-peas under cold running water. Put them in a large, heavy-bottomed saucepan and pour in enough cold water to cover them by about 5 cm (2 inches). Discard any chick-peas that float to the surface. Cover the saucepan, leaving the lid ajar, and bring the water to the boil; cook for 2 minutes. Turn off the heat, cover the pan, and soak the chick-peas for at least 1 hour. Alternatively, soak the chick-peas overnight in cold water.

When the chick-peas have finished soaking, drain them well in a colander. Return them to the pan and pour in enough water to cover them by about 5 cm (2 inches). Bring the liquid to a simmer; cook the chickpeas over medium-low heat until they are quite tender—45 minutes to 1 hour. (Add more water if they look to be drying out) When cooked, drain the peas and allow to cool.

Place the chick-peas in a food processor with the tahini, yogurt, garlic, lemon juice, salt and some freshly ground pepper. Process for about 45 seconds to produce a soft, creamy paste. Turn the dip into a shallow bowl and sprinkle with some paprika and chopped parsley before serving.

Salmon-Filled Choux Buns

Serves 6

Working (and total) time: about 1 hour and 30 minutes

Calories 225
Protein 12g
Cholesterol 90mg
Total fat 13g
Saturated fat 4g
Sodium 295mg

60 cl	unsalted fish stock	**1 pint**	**15 g**	polyunsaturated margarine, chilled and cubed	**½ oz**
15 cl	dry white wine	**¼ pint**		**Choux dough**	
⅛ tsp	salt	**⅛ tsp**	**45 g**	polyunsaturated margarine	**1½ oz**
	freshly ground black pepper		**75 g**	plain flour, sifted	**1½ oz**
175 g	salmon tail, skinned, filleted and cut into six equal portions	**6 oz**	**2**	eggs, beaten	**2**
175 g	fine French beans	**6 oz**	**30 g**	smoked salmon, finely chopped	**1 oz**
½	small lemon, juice only	**½**	**1 tbsp**	finely chopped fresh dill	**1 tbsp**

Preheat the oven to 200°C (400°F or Mark 6). To make the choux dough, put the margarine in a small saucepan with 12.5 cl (4 fl oz) of water, and bring it to the boil over medium heat. Remove from the heat and quickly beat in the flour. Return it to a low heat and cook for about 1 minute to dry it out a little.

Remove the pan from the heat and slowly add the beaten eggs. Stir in the salmon and dill.

Grease a baking sheet and spoon on the choux mixture, forming six small piles. Bake until golden—about 25 to 30 minutes.

Combine 45 cl (¾ pint) of the fish stock with the white wine and boil to reduce it by two thirds. Season with the salt and some pepper, stir in the lemon juice, and set aside.

When the buns are cooked, slit them to form six lids and six bases. Keep warm.

Poach the salmon fillet pieces in the remaining fish stock until they turn pale pink.

Boil the French beans until they are cooked but still crunchy. Set aside and keep warm.

Gently reheat the fish stock and wine mixture and whisk in the margarine cubes to thicken it. Keep warm.

Place one portion of the poached salmon fillet in each choux bun. Toss the French beans in the sauce and serve them alongside.

Mushroom Strudel

Serves 6

**Working time:
about 40
minutes**

**Total time:
about 1 hour
and 30
minutes
(includes
cooling)**

**Calories
130
Protein
5g
Cholesterol
5mg
Total fat
5g
Saturated fat
2g
Sodium
130mg**

2 tsp	virgin olive oil	**2 tsp**
1	large onion, finely chopped	**1**
2	garlic cloves, crushed	**2**
500 g	open mushrooms, chopped	**1 lb**
2 tsp	chopped fresh marjoram	**2 tsp**
1 tsp	Dijon mustard	**1 tsp**
125 g	fresh wholemeal breadcrumbs	**4 oz**
½ tsp	salt	**½ tsp**
	freshly grated nutmeg	
	freshly ground black pepper	
4	sheets phyllo pastry, each about	**4**
	45 by 30 cm (18 by 12 inches)	
15 g	unsalted butter, melted	**½ oz**

Heat the oil in a heavy saucepan and gently cook the onion and garlic in the olive oil until the onion has softened. Increase the heat, add the mushrooms, and cook, stirring, until they release their juices. Put the mushroom pulp to one side of the pan, then boil the juices rapidly until they have evaporated. Stir the marjoram, mustard, breadcrumbs, salt and some nutmeg and black pepper into the pulp, and set the mixture aside to cool completely.

Preheat the oven to 200°C (400°F or Mark 6). Lay one sheet of phyllo pastry on the work surface and brush it with a little of the melted butter. Lay a second sheet of pastry on top and brush it with a little more of the butter.

Repeat the process with the third and fourth sheets of phyllo. Spoon the mushroom filling down the long side of pastry nearest to you, about 5 cm (2 inches) in from the edge, and pack it down lightly with the back of the spoon to form a sausage shape about 2.5 cm (1 inch) in diameter. Working away from you, roll up the filling inside the pastry. Using two metal spatulas, transfer the strudel to a large, lightly oiled baking sheet. Brush with the remaining butter and sprinkle with a little grated nutmeg. Bake it in the oven for 20 to 25 minutes, until it is crisp and golden.

Leave it to cool completely before cutting it into slices and serving.

Individual Smoked Trout Flans

Make 6 flans

Working time:
about 25
minutes

Total time:
about 1 hour
and 10
minutes

Per flan:
Calories
160
Protein
22g
Cholesterol
55mg
Total fat
15g
Saturated fat
3g
Sodium
210mg

175 g	wholemeal flour	**6 oz**
90 g	polyunsaturated margarine, chilled	**3 oz**
400 g	skinned smoked trout fillets	**14 oz**
15 cl	skimmed milk	**¼ pint**
3 tbsp	grated horseradish	**3 tbsp**
125 g	fromage frais	**4 oz**
125 g	cucumber, peeled and diced	**4 oz**

1 tbsp	chopped fresh tarragon	**1 tbsp**
1	lemon, finely grated rind and juice	**1**
	freshly ground black pepper	
2	egg whites	**2**
6	lemon wedges, for garnish	**6**
6	tarragon sprigs, for garnish	**6**

Put the flour into a bowl and rub in the margarine, until the mixture resembles fine breadcrumbs. Using a round-bladed knife, stir in 3 tablespoons of water to make a firm dough. Turn the dough on to a lightly floured surface and knead it until smooth. Divide the dough into six portions. Roll out the portions thinly and use them to line six fluted flan cases about 10 cm (4 inches) in diameter and 2.5 cm (1 inch) deep. Prick the cases all over with a fork and chill for 20 minutes while you preheat the oven to 200°C (400°F or Mark 6).

Meanwhile, place the trout fillets in a large saucepan with the milk, and poach them until tender—about 15 minutes. Drain and set aside.

Bake the chilled flan cases for 20 to 25 minutes. Reduce the oven temperature to 170°C (325°F or Mark 3).

Flake the flesh of the smoked trout and put it in a bowl. Mix in the horseradish, fromage frais, cucumber, chopped tarragon, the lemon rind and juice and some black pepper.

In a separate bowl, whisk the egg whites until they begin to form soft peaks then fold them into the fish mixture. Fill the pastry cases with the filling and bake the flans until they are set—about 15 minutes. Allow the flans to cool, then refrigerate until required.

Serve each one garnished with a lemon wedge and a sprig of tarragon.

Asparagus and Walnut Frittata

Serves 6

Working and (total time): about 30 minutes

Calories 150
Protein 10g
Cholesterol 120mg
Total fat 10g
Saturated fat 3g
Sodium 205mg

300 g	asparagus, trimmed	**10 oz**		**60 g**	day-old wholemeal bread, crusts	**2 oz**
3	eggs	**3**			removed, soaked for 10 minutes in	
3	egg whites	**3**			4 tbsp skimmed milk	
45 g	grated Parmesan cheese	**1½ oz**		**⅛ tsp**	salt	**⅛ tsp**
1 tbsp	chopped fresh basil	**1 tbsp**			freshly ground black pepper	
45 g	shelled walnuts, toasted, chopped	**1½ oz**		**1 tsp**	virgin olive or safflower oil	**1 tsp**

Bring a large, shallow pan of water to the boil. Cook the asparagus in the boiling water for about 2 minutes, then drain it, refresh it under cold running water, and drain it again well. Cut the asparagus into 5 cm (2 inch) pieces and set them aside.

Whisk the whole eggs and egg whites with the Parmesan and the chopped walnuts. Add the soaked bread, the basil and the asparagus pieces to the egg mixture, and season it with the salt and some black pepper. Mix the ingredients well.

Heat the oil in a non-stick frying pan over medium heat and pour in the egg mixture; distribute the asparagus pieces evenly in the frying pan and flatten the mixture with the back of a wooden spoon. Cook the frittata over medium heat for 5 to 8 minutes, until the underside is firm. Invert the frittata on to a large plate, then slide it back into the frying pan and cook the second side until it, too, is firm and golden-brown—another 5 to 8 minutes. Slide the frittata back on to the plate.

The frittata may be served cold or hot, cut into wedges.

Marinated Steak Salad with Vegetable Batons

Serves 6

Working time: about 45 minutes

Total time: about 6 hours (includes marinating)

Calories 290
Protein 34g
Cholesterol 80mg
Total fat 13g
Saturated fat 5g
Sodium 110mg

1 tbsp	safflower oil	1 tbsp
800 g	beef fillet, trimmed	1 lb 10 oz
1	1 cm (½ inch) piece fresh ginger root, finely chopped	1
2	garlic cloves, crushed	2
5 tbsp	rice wine or sherry	5 tbsp

3 tbsp	soy sauce or shoyu	3 tbsp
	freshly ground black pepper	
250 g	carrots	8 oz
½	cucumber	½
2	sticks celery	2
250 g	canned bamboo shoots	8 oz

Preheat the oven to 220°C (425°F or Mark 7).

Pour the oil into a large, shallow fireproof casserole or roasting pan set over high heat. Sear the meat until it is well browned on all sides—3 to 5 minutes. Place the casserole in the oven and cook the fillet for 15 minutes for rare meat, or for up to 30 minutes for medium meat. Remove the fillet from the oven and let it rest and cool for 30 minutes.

In a shallow, rigid container, mix together the ginger, garlic, rice wine, soy sauce and a grinding of black pepper, to make a marinade. Slice the meat as thinly as possible across the grain, and place the slices in the marinade. Cover the container with a lid or with foil and leave the meat to marinate in the refrigerator for at least 4 hours, or overnight, turning it from time to time.

Cut the carrots, cucumber, celery and bamboo shoots into 4 to 5 cm (1½ to 2 inch) batons. Mix the prepared vegetables together.

Transfer the vegetables to individual plates. Lift the slices of fillet from the marinade and lay them over the salad.

Spiced Fillet of Beef

Serves 12

Working time:
about 1 hour

Total time:
about 7 hours
and
30 minutes
(includes
cooling and
chilling)

Calories
290

Protein
30g

Cholesterol
65mg

Total fat
14g

Saturated fat
5g

Sodium
240mg

45 g	pine-nuts	**1½ oz**
2 tbsp	virgin olive oil	**2 tbsp**
1	large onion, finely chopped	**1**
3	garlic cloves, crushed	**3**
2 tsp	ground coriander	**2 tsp**
1½ tsp	ground cardamom	**1½ tsp**
1 tsp	ground cumin	**1 tsp**
3 tsp	paprika	**3 tsp**

1¼ tsp	salt	**1¼ tsp**
⅛ tsp	cayenne pepper	**⅛ tsp**
	freshly ground black pepper	
150 g	seedless raisins	**5 oz**
250 g	chestnut mushrooms, chopped	**8 oz**
1.5 kg	beef fillet, trimmed	**3 lb**
2 tbsp	black peppercorns, crushed	**2 tbsp**
4 tbsp	finely chopped parsley	**4 tbsp**

Brown the pine-nuts in a dry frying pan for 30 seconds. Heat 1 tablespoon of the oil in a frying pan and cook the onion until soft—about 5 minutes. Stir in the garlic, cumin, coriander, cardamom, 2 teaspoons paprika, ¾ teaspoon salt, the cayenne and plenty black pepper. Cook for 2 minutes, then stir in the raisins and mushrooms. Cook for 10 to 15 minutes, until the raisins are plump. Remove the pan from the heat, add the pine-nuts and allow to cool.

Preheat the oven to 220°C (425°F or Mark 7). Make an incision in the fillet by inserting a carving knife into the meat from the middle of one end, and pressing it in as far as possible.

Insert a sharpening steel into the slit and make a hole 2.5 to 5 cm (1 to 2 inches) wide.

Carefully push the cooled stuffing into the fillet and tie with string at 2.5 cm (1 inch) intervals. Season with the remaining salt and coat it evenly with the crushed peppercorns.

Heat the remaining tablespoon of oil in a roasting pan and brown the fillet all over. Transfer the roasting pan to the oven and cook for 30 minutes, basting frequently.

Allow the fillet to cool, then refrigerate it, covered, for at least 4 hours. Coat the meat with the chopped parsley and sprinkle with the remaining paprika before serving.

Seafood and Tagliatelle Salad

Serves 8

Working time:
about 45
minutes

Total time:
about 1 hour

Calories
315
Protein
26g
Cholesterol
300mg
Total fat
7g
Saturated fat
1g
Sodium
420mg

1 kg	baby squid, cleaned and skinned, tentacles reserved	2 lb
12 tsp	white wine vinegar	12 tsp
12	peppercorns	12
2	bay leaves	2
1 tsp	salt	1 tsp
350 g	green tagliatelle	12 oz
250 g	peeled cooked prawns	8 oz
1	sweet red pepper, seeded, and cut into long julienne	1

8	large cooked prawns, peeled, for garnish	8
	Lemon vinaigrette	
¼ tsp	salt	¼ tsp
2½ tbsp	fresh lemon juice	2½ tbsp
½	lemon, grated rind only	½
3 tbsp	virgin olive oil	3 tbsp
¼	garlic clove, finely chopped	¼
¼ tsp	chili pepper, finely chopped	¼ tsp
2 tbsp	chopped parsley	2 tbsp

For the vinaigrette, put all the ingredients into a screw-top jar and shake well to combine them. Refrigerate until required.

Slice the squid pouches into rings, and cut the tentacles in half crosswise. Bring 1 litre (2 pints) of water to the boil in a saucepan with the vinegar, peppercorns, bay leaves and salt. Add the squid to the pan, and cook it in the boiling water for 2 minutes. Drain well, and set aside to cool; discard the bay leaves and peppercorns.

Add the tagliatelle to 3 litres (5 pints) of boiling water with 1 teaspoon of salt. Start testing the pasta after 10 minutes, and cook it until it is *al dente*. Drain, and rinse under cold running water, then drain it again. Place the squid, pasta, small prawns, red pepper strips and vinaigrette in a large bowl, and toss them until they are thoroughly combined.

Turn the salad on to a platter and serve garnished with the large prawns.

Artichoke Filled with Seafood in a Dill Dressing

Serves 4

Working time:
about 1 hour

Total time:
about 4 hours
(includes
marinating)

Calories
230

Protein
28g

Cholesterol
100mg

Total fat
11g

Saturated fat
3g

Sodium
480mg

1	garlic clove, halved	**1**
3 tbsp	fresh lemon juice	**3 tbsp**
4	globe artichokes	**4**
250 g	salmon trout fillets	**8 oz**
4	shelled scallops, bright white connective tissue removed	**4**
1	shallot	**1**
3 tbsp	dry vermouth	**3 tbsp**

1 tsp	safflower oil	**1 tsp**
	freshly ground black pepper	
2	fresh thyme sprigs	**2**
125 g	white crab meat, flaked	**4 oz**
2 tsp	chopped fresh dill	**2 tsp**
1	lemon, finely grated rind of half, the other half sliced, for garnish	**1**
4	thin slices smoked salmon	**4**

Pour 4 litres (7 pints) of water into a large saucepan and add the garlic and 1 tablespoon of the lemon juice. Cut off and discard the top third and the stem of each artichoke. Trim and rinse them, then simmer them for 40 to 45 minutes in the acidulated water until tender.

Preheat the oven to 190°C (375°F or Mark 5), and lightly grease a large sheet of foil. Wrap the trout fillets and scallops in the foil with the shallot, 1 tablespoon of the lemon juice, 2 tablespoons of the vermouth, the oil, some pepper and the thyme. Place the parcel on a baking sheet and put it in the oven for 15 minutes. Leave the fish to cool in its parcel.

Once cooked, flake the trout into a bowl. Add the scallops and the crab meat. Strain the reserved cooking liquid and mix into it the remaining lemon juice and vermouth, the dill and the lemon rind. Add this to the fish and toss the ingredients lightly. Cover the bowl and marinate for at least 2 hours.

Form the smoked salmon slices into neat rolls. Remove the choke from each cooled artichoke and spoon in the fish mixture. Top each one with a smoked salmon roll. Cover the filled artichokes loosely with plastic film and chill them until required.

Serve garnished with lemon slices.

Cottage Cheese, Prawn and Pepper Sandwiches

Makes 6
sandwiches

Working
(and total)
time: about
25 minutes

Per sandwich:
Calories
160
Protein
12g
Cholesterol
30mg
Total fat
3g
Saturated fat
1g
Sodium
450mg

200 g	low-fat cottage cheese	7 oz	6	button mushrooms,	6
1 tbsp	tomato paste	1 tbsp		wiped clean and thinly sliced	
	white pepper		$\frac{1}{2}$	sweet red pepper, seeded,	$\frac{1}{2}$
12	slices wholegrain bread	12		deribbed and sliced into six rings	
90 g	peeled cooked prawns	3 oz	6	chives finely cut	6

Place the cottage cheese in a bowl and stir in the tomato paste and some white pepper. Spread the cheese mixture evenly over six of the sliced of bread, and divide the prawns, sliced mushrooms and pepper rings among the covered slices. Scatter some cut chives over each filling, and press a second slice of bread gently on top.

24

Chinese-Style Beef Sandwiches

Makes 6
sandwiches

Working
(and total)
time: about
30 minutes

Per sandwich:
Calories
335
Protein
16g
Cholesterol
20mg
Total fat
14g
Saturated fat
4g
Sodium
480mg

1	granary baguette, about 60 cm (2 feet) long, cut into six	1	6	slices cold cooked lean beef	6
45 g	polyunsaturated margarine	1½ oz	1	slice fresh pineapple	1
1½ tsp	finely chopped fresh ginger root	1½ tsp	45 g	skinned peanuts, chopped	1½ oz
2 tbsp	soy sauce or shoyu	2 tbsp	3	spring onions, trimmed, white parts sliced, green parts cut lengthwise into slivers	3

Cut open the baguette pieces. In a small bowl, stir together the margarine, ginger root and soy sauce, and spread this mixture evenly over the bottoms of the baguette pieces. Place a slice of beef loosely on each covered base, then cover them with the chopped pineapple and peanuts, and the spring onions. Replace the top halves of the baguette pieces.

Avocado and Mozzarella Salad in Rye Bread

Makes 6
sandwiches

Working
(and total)
time: about
25 minutes

Per sandwich:
Calories
225
Protein
8g
Cholesterol
5mg
Total fat
6g
Saturated fat
2g
Sodium
400mg

1	small avocado, halved, stoned and peeled	1	45 g	low-fat mozzarella sliced	1½ oz	
2 tbsp	fresh lemon juice	2 tbsp	1	large tomato, halved, seeded and sliced	1	
	white pepper		1	small onion, cut into rings	1	
6	fresh basil leaves, shredded	6	1	black olive, stoned and thinly sliced	1	
12	slices dark rye bread	12				

Put the avocado flesh in a bowl and mash it with a fork. Add the fresh lemon juice, and some white pepper together with the shredded basil leaves and mix them in thoroughly with the fork.

Spread six pieces of bread evenly with the avocado mixture, then top each one with some of the cheese, tomato, onion and olive slices. Press a second piece of bread gently on to each filled base.

Chicken and Pickled Walnut Mousses

Serves 4

Working time:
about 35
minutes

Total time:
about 3 hours
and
15 minutes
(includes
chilling)

Calories
225
Protein
37g
Cholesterol
90mg
Total fat
7g
Saturated fat
2g
Sodium
195mg

4	chicken breasts, skinned, boned and sliced	**4**
1	onion, coarsely chopped	**1**
15 cl	plain low-fat yogurt	**¼ pint**
1	garlic clove, crushed	**1**
¼ tsp	ground coriander	**¼ tsp**
⅛ tsp	salt	**⅛ tsp**
	freshly ground black pepper	
2	egg whites	**2**
4	pickled walnuts, two coarsely chopped, two halved for garnish	**4**

Preheat the oven to 180°C (350°F or Mark 4). Lightly oil four ramekin dishes.

Put half of the chicken and half of the onion into a food processor and process them until they are completely smooth. Transfer the purée to a bowl, then process the remaining chicken and onion and add it to the bowl. Add the yogurt, garlic, coriander, salt and some freshly ground black pepper, and beat the mixture until it is smooth.

In a separate bowl, whisk the egg whites until they form stiff peaks. Stir 2 tablespoons of the egg whites into the chicken purée to loosen the mixture, then, using a wooden spoon, fold in the remainder.

Half-fill each ramekin with the chicken mousse. Sprinkle chopped walnuts equally into each ramekin and fill up with the remaining mousse.

Stand the ramekins in a baking pan and pour in sufficient boiling water to come two thirds of the way up the sides of the ramekins. Place the baking pan in the oven and bake the mousses for 35 to 40 minutes, or until they are firm to the touch. Remove the ramekins from the pan and allow them to cool to room temperature, then chill them for at least 2 hours.

To serve, run a knife round the edge of each ramekin, and carefully turn the mousses out on to serving plates. Garnish the top of each one with a pickled walnut half.

Summer Beans with Fettuccine and Basil

Serves 2

Working
(and total)
time: about
1 hour and
15 minutes

Calories
350
Protein
14g
Cholesterol
75mg
Total fat
14g
Saturated fat
4g
Sodium
265mg

125 g	fettucine	**4 oz**
15 cl	unsalted vegetable stock	**¼ pint**
500 g	fresh broad beans, shelled, coarse outer skins removed	**1 lb**
60 g	French beans, trimmed and cut into short lengths	**2 oz**
60 g	mange-tout, strings removed	**2 oz**

60 ml	single cream	**2 fl oz**
1 tbsp	toasted sesame seeds, ground	**1 tbsp**
½	garlic clove, crushed	**½**
2 tbsp	chopped fresh basil, plus basil sprigs for garnish	**2 tbsp**
¼ tsp	salt	**¼ tsp**
	freshly ground black pepper	

To make the sauce, bring the vegetable stock to the boil in a heavy-bottomed saucepan and add the broad beans. Reduce the heat and simmer the beans for 5 minutes. Add the French beans and simmer for 3 to 4 minutes, until just tender. Add the mange-tout and simmer for a further minute. Reserving the stock, drain the vegetables and keep them warm. Return the stock to the pan and reduce it to 90 ml (3 fl oz) by fast boiling, then set it aside while you prepare the fettuccine.

Add the fettuccine to 1½ litres (2½ pints) of boiling water with ¾ teaspoon of salt. Cook until it is *al dente*. Drain the pasta and keep it warm.

Stir the cream, ground sesame seeds, garlic, basil, salt and a generous amount of freshly ground black pepper into the reduced stock. Add the beans, mange-tout and freshly cooked pasta, and toss carefully over low heat until warmed through. Serve garnished with sprigs of fresh basil.

Kohlrabi and Courgette Gratin

Serves 4

Working time: about 35 minutes

Total time: about 1 hour and 10 minutes

Calories 145

Protein 8g

Cholesterol 15mg

Total fat 7g

Saturated fat 4g

Sodium 415mg

750 g	kohlrabi, leaves and stems removed, unpeeled if young	1½ lb
250 g	courgettes, trimmed	8 oz
30 g	unsalted butter	1 oz
500 g	tomatoes, skinned, seeded and chopped	1 lb

2 tbsp	finely chopped parsley	2 tbsp
2	garlic cloves, crushed	2
⅛ tsp	cayenne pepper	⅛ tsp
!stsp	salt	!stsp
	freshly ground black pepper	
30 g	fresh wholemeal breadcrumbs	1 oz

Using a sharp knife or a mandolin, cut the kohlrabi horizontally into very thin, even slices. Cut the courgettes lengthwise into equally thin slices. Put the kohlrabi slices in a steamer set over a pan of boiling water and steam for 15 minutes, then add the courgette slices to the steamer. Keep the two vegetables separate. Continue to cook the vegetables until both are just tender—another 5 to 10 minutes.

Meanwhile, melt the butter in a heavy-bottomed saucepan over low heat. Add the tomatoes, parsley and garlic, and season the mixture with the cayenne pepper, salt and some black pepper. Stir the ingredients well and cook them over medium heat for 10 to 15 minutes, stirring occasionally, until the tomatoes have reduced to a fairly thick, dry purée.

Preheat the oven to 180°C (350°F or Mark 4). Grease a round or oval gratin dish.

Drain the kohlrabi and courgette slices and pat them dry with paper towels. Arrange alternate layers of kohlrabi and courgette slices in the prepared gratin dish. Spoon the tomato purée over the top and sprinkle on the breadcrumbs. Put the dish in the oven and bake the gratin for 20 to 30 minutes, until the topping is crisp and lightly browned.

Leeks and Cheese in Phyllo Packets

Serves 6

Working time: about 45 minutes

Total time: about 1 hour and 45 minutes

Calories 275

Protein 9g

Cholesterol 30mg

Total fat 14g

Saturated fat 6g

Sodium 290mg

4	medium leeks, trimmed, cleaned, sliced into 1 cm (½ inch) pieces	**4**
1 tbsp	safflower oil	**1 tbsp**
30 g	unsalted butter	**1 oz**
275 g	onion, chopped	**9 oz**
1	garlic clove, finely chopped	**1**
¼ tsp	dried thyme	**¼ tsp**
¼ tsp	salt	**¼ tsp**
	freshly ground black pepper	
2 tbsp	single cream	**2 tbsp**
150 g	Gruyère or other Swiss cheese, grated	**5 oz**
12	sheets phyllo pastry, each 30 cm (12 inches) square	**12**

In a large, heavy frying pan, heat the oil and half the butter over medium heat. Add the leeks, onion, garlic, thyme, salt and pepper. Cook, stirring often, for 12 minutes. Stir in the cream and continue cooking until all the liquid is absorbed—about 3 minutes more.

Transfer the leek mixture to a bowl and let it cool slightly. Stir in the cheese and refrigerate the mixture for 30 minutes.

Preheat the oven to 180°C (350°F or Mark 4). On a clean, dry work surface, lay out two sheets of phyllo dough, one on top of the other. Mound about one sixth of the leek-cheese mixture 7.5 cm (3 inches) from the lower right corner of the dough. Fold up the dough to form a compact packet. Repeat the process with the remaining filling and dough sheets to form six packets in all. Put the packets, seam sides down, on a lightly buttered baking sheet. Melt the remaining butter in a small saucepan over low heat. Brush the packets with the melted butter and bake them until they are golden—about 30 minutes. Serve them hot.

Jacket Potatoes with Cream, Broccoli and Asparagus

Serves 4

Working time: about 15 minutes

Total time: about 40 minutes

Calories 280
Protein 8g
Cholesterol 25mg
Total fat 9g
Saturated fat 5g
Sodium 135mg

4	large potatoes, scrubbed well, pricked all over with a fork	**4**	
250 g	broccoli	**8 oz**	
125 g	asparagus	**4 oz**	
1 tsp	olive oil	**1 tsp**	
15 cl	soured cream	**¼ pint**	
¼ tsp	salt	**¼ tsp**	
	freshly ground black pepper		
	finely cut chives		
	paprika for garnish		

Peel the broccoli stalks right up to the heads. Cut off the heads and divide them into small florets. Cut the stalks diagonally into thin slices. Thinly peel the asparagus up to the tips. Cut off the tips, then slice the stems.

Put the broccoli and asparagus into a bowl with 2 tablespoons of cold water. Cover with plastic film, leaving a corner open. Microwave on full power until the vegetables are just tender—2½ to 3 minutes—stirring twice during cooking. Remove and set aside.

Rub the skins of the potatoes with the olive oil. Place on kitchen paper in the microwave. Microwave on high until they are cooked through—about 20 minutes—turning them over half way through cooking.

Put the soured cream into a bowl and season with the salt and pepper. Stir in the chives, broccoli and asparagus. Cut the potatoes almost in half diagonally, and arrange on a serving dish. Microwave the soured cream mixture for 1 minute, then spoon some into each potato. Sprinkle with paprika and serve.

Turkey Salad with Feta Cheese

Serves 2

Working time:
about 20
minutes

Total time:
about 20
minutes

Calories
495
Protein
42g
Cholesterol
105mg
Total fat
33g
Saturated fat
8g
Sodium
710mg

250 g	cooked turkey breast meat, skinned and cubed	**8 oz**
½	small cucumber, peeled, halved, seeded and sliced diagonally	½
4	red radishes, diced	4
4	large Greek black olives, stoned and halved	4
60 g	feta cheese, cut into cubes	**2 oz**
250 g	fresh spinach, stemmed, washed and dried	**8 oz**

	Basil vinaigrette	
1	garlic clove, finely chopped	**1**
1 tbsp	chopped fresh basil, or 2 tsp dried basil	**1 tbsp**
¼ **tsp**	sugar	¼ **tsp**
½ **tbsp**	grainy mustard freshly ground black pepper	½ **tbsp**
1 tbsp	fresh lemon juice	**1 tbsp**
1 tbsp	red wine vinegar	**1 tbsp**
1 tbsp	safflower oil	**1 tbsp**
2 tbsp	virgin olive oil	**2 tbsp**

To prepare the vinaigrette, place all the ingredients in a screw-top jar with a tight-fitting lid and shake vigorously until thoroughly blended—about 30 seconds.

Combine the turkey, cucumber, radishes, olives and cheese in a large bowl, add the dressing, and toss. Arrange the spinach on plates and spoon the salad on top.

Chicken with Peanuts and Ginger Sauce

Serves 6

Working time:
about 20
minutes

Total time:
about 2 hours
and
20 minutes

Calories
260

Protein
30g

Cholesterol
70mg

Total fat
12g

Saturated fat
3g

Sodium
200mg

750 g	chicken breast meat, cubed	**1½ lb**	**¼ litre**	unsalted chicken stock	**8 fl oz**
12.5 cl	dry white wine	**4 fl oz**	**2 tbsp**	peanut butter	**2 tbsp**
45 g	fresh ginger, finely chopped	**1½ oz**	**1 tsp**	tomato paste (optional)	**1 tsp**
1	garlic clove, crushed	**1**	**2**	spring onions, julienned	**2**
¼ tsp	salt	**¼ tsp**	**45 g**	peanuts, crushed	**1½ oz**
	freshly ground black pepper		**1 tbsp**	safflower oil	**1 tbsp**

Make a marinade of the wine, ginger, garlic, salt and pepper, and let the chicken stand in it for 2 hours.

Near the end of the marinating time, prepare the sauce. Pour the stock into a small saucepan and whisk in the peanut butter and the tomato paste, if used. Add the spring onions and simmer the sauce over low heat, uncovered, for 2 minutes. Remove the saucepan from the heat and set it aside.

Remove the cubes from the marinade and set them aside. Strain the marinade and add it to the sauce. Return the mixture to a simmer and cook over low heat, stirring occasionally, until the sauce is thick enough to coat the back of a spoon—about 4 minutes. Remove the pan from the heat.

Roll the chicken cubes in the crushed peanuts, sparsely coating the cubes. Heat the oil in a heavy frying pan over high heat. When the oil is hot but not smoking, add the chicken cubes and lightly brown them, stirring gently to keep intact as much of the peanut coating as possible— about 3 minutes. Remove the frying pan from the heat and allow the chicken to finish cooking as it rests in the hot pan—about 2 minutes more. Transfer the chicken to a warmed platter and pour the sauce over it just before serving.

Prawn and French Bean Salad

Serves 4

Working time:
about 30
minutes

Total time:
about 1 hour

Calories
185
Protein
20g
Cholesterol
135mg
Total fat
6g
Saturated fat
1g
Sodium
235mg

500 g	prawns, shells left on	**1 lb**	**¼ tsp**	salt	**¼ tsp**
750 g	French beans, trimmed, and cut in half	**1½ lb**		freshly ground black pepper	
			12.5 cl	plain low-fat yogurt	**4 fl oz**
1½ tbsp	tarragon vinegar	**1½ tbsp**	**1 tbsp**	soured cream	**1 tbsp**
1 tbsp	safflower oil	**1 tbsp**	**1½ tsp**	Dijon mustard	**1½ tsp**
2 tbsp	chopped fresh tarragon, or 2 tsp dried tarragon	**2 tbsp**	**1 tsp**	tomato paste	**1 tsp**
2 tbsp	finely cut chives	**2 tbsp**	**1 tbsp**	chopped fresh parsley	**1 tbsp**

Bring 2 litres (3½ pints) of water to the boil in a large saucepan. Add the beans and boil them until they are just tender—about 6 minutes. Drain the beans and refresh them under cold running water. Transfer them to a bowl. Set the bowl aside.

If the prawns are raw, bring 1 litre (1¾ pints) of water to a simmer in the saucepan. Add the prawns, cover the pan, and simmer the prawns until they are opaque—2 to 3 minutes. Drain them and let them cool enough to handle. Peel the prawns (and, if you like, devein them). Add the prawns to the beans.

In a small bowl, whisk together the vinegar, oil, half of the tarragon, 1 tablespoon of the chives, ⅛ teaspoon of the salt and some pepper. Arrange the prawns and beans on a serving platter and spoon the vinegar-and-oil marinade over it. Let the dish marinate at room temperature for 30 minutes.

Near the end of the marinating time, prepare the dressing: whisk together the yogurt, soured cream, mustard and tomato paste. Stir in the parsley, the remaining tarragon and the remaining chives, the remaining salt and some pepper. Pour the dressing into a small serving bowl and serve it with the salad.

Stir-Fried Squid with Asparagus and Mushrooms

Serves 4

Working time: about 35 minutes

Total time: about 45 minutes

Calories 230
Protein 20g
Cholesterol 265mg
Total fat 8g
Saturated fat 1g
Sodium 565mg

750 g	squid, cleaned	1½ lb
8	dried Chinese mushrooms, covered with ¼ litre (8 fl oz) boiling water and soaked for 20 minutes	8
2 tbsp	rice wine	2 tbsp
2	garlic cloves, finely chopped	2
250 g	asparagus, trimmed and sliced diagonally into short lengths	8 oz

4	spring onions, trimmed and thinly sliced diagonally	4
1 tbsp	low-sodium soy sauce or shoyu	1 tbsp
1 tbsp	rice vinegar	1 tbsp
1 tbsp	fermented black beans, rinsed and mashed	1 tbsp
2 tsp	cornflour	2 tsp
2 tbsp	safflower oil	2 tbsp

Remove the mushrooms from their soaking liquid and set them aside. Carefully pour the liquid into a small saucepan. Boil it until it is reduced to 4 tablespoons. Set aside. Stem the mushrooms and slice each one into quarters.

Slit the squid pouches and flatten them on a work surface. With a knife, score the inside surface of each pouch in a crosshatch pattern. Cut the pouches into 2.5 cm (1 inch) squares. Combine the squares and the tentacles with the rice wine and the garlic. Marinate the squid in this mixture for 15 minutes.

Drain the squid, reserving the marinade. Heat 1 tablespoon of the safflower oil in a wok. Add half of the squid pieces and stir-fry them until the squares are tightly curled—about 2 minutes. Remove and set aside. Heat ½ tablespoon of the oil in the wok and stir fry the second batch of squid; set aside.

Stir-fry the mushrooms, asparagus and spring onions for 2 minutes. Add the fermented black beans, vinegar, and the reserved marinade and cook for 1 minute longer.

Combine the reduced mushroom-soaking liquid and the cornflour, and pour the mixture into the wok. Stir the vegetables until the sauce has thickened. Combine the squid with the vegetables and stir. Serve at once.

Crab-Stuffed Mushroom Caps

Serves 12

Working time: about 25 minutes

Total time: about 50 minutes

Calories 100

Protein 8g

Cholesterol 20mg

Total fat 4g

Saturated fat 2g

Sodium 135mg

250 g	crab meat, picked over	**8 oz**
35 cl	fish stock	**12 fl oz**
1	lemon, juice only	**1**
36	large mushrooms, stems removed and chopped	**36**
2 tbsp	finely chopped shallot	**2 tbsp**
12.5 cl	dry vermouth	**4 fl oz**
2 tsp	fresh thyme	**2 tsp**
15 g	unsalted butter	**½ oz**

2 tbsp	flour	**2 tbsp**
17.5 cl	semi-skimmed milk	**6 fl oz**
⅛ tsp	salt	**⅛ tsp**
	grated nutmeg	
	white pepper	
60 g	Parmesan cheese, freshly grated	**2 oz**
15 g	fresh basil, coarsely chopped	**½ oz**
2 tbsp	pistachio nuts, crushed	**2 tbsp**

In a large frying pan, heat ¼ litre (8 fl oz) of the stock and the lemon juice over medium heat. Add the mushroom caps and toss them gently to coat them. Cover the pan and poach the mushrooms, turning occasionally, until they are cooked through—6 to 7 minutes.

Transfer the mushrooms to a platter lined with paper towels. Add the shallot to the pan along with the chopped mushroom stems, the vermouth and the thyme. Bring to the boil, then simmer until all but 2 tablespoons of the liquid has evaporated. Set aside.

Melt the butter in a small saucepan and whisk in the flour to form a paste. Cook the paste for 3 minutes, stirring constantly Slowly pour in the milk, then the remaining stock. Add the salt, some nutmeg and white pepper. Simmer the sauce until it thickens then stir in the cheese and the basil.

Preheat the grill. Combine the crab meat with the mushroom mixture in a bowl. Slowly pour the sauce into the bowl and stir gently. Mound tablespoons of stuffing in the hollow of each mushroom. Grill the mushrooms until the crab begins to brown—about 3 minutes. Sprinkle on the pistachios and serve hot.

Meat Loaf with Olives

Serves 6

Working time: about 15 minutes

Total time: about 30 minutes

Calories 275

Protein 32g

Cholesterol 85mg

Total fat 12g

Saturated fat 5g

Sodium 320mg

850 g	lean lamb, minced	1¾ lb
1	egg white, lightly beaten	1
1 tbsp	chopped fresh oregano, or 1 tsp dried oregano	1 tbsp
¼ tsp	cayenne pepper	¼ tsp
2	garlic cloves, finely chopped	2
4 tbsp	finely chopped onion	4 tbsp

30 g	parsley, chopped	1 oz
6	oil-cured black olives, stoned and finely chopped	6
60 g	dry breadcrumbs	2 oz
4 tbsp	grated Parmesan cheese	4 tbsp
1 tbsp	red wine vinegar	1 tbsp
1½ tbsp	tomato paste	1½ tbsp

In a large bowl, combine the egg white, oregano, cayenne pepper, garlic and onion. Add the lamb, parsley, olives, breadcrumbs, Parmesan cheese, vinegar and 1 tablespoon of the tomato paste. Using a wooden spoon, mix all the ingredients together.

Shape the meat mixture into a log about 7.5 cm (3 inches) in diameter. Place the log in a shallow baking dish and spread the remaining ½ tablespoon of tomato paste over the surface of the meat. Microwave the loaf, uncovered, on high for 10 to 12 minutes, rotating the dish a half turn midway through the cooking time. Let the meat loaf stand for 10 minutes. To serve, cut the loaf into 12 slices.

Mediterranean Courgettes

Serves 4

Working (and total) time: about 30 minutes

Calories 160
Protein 20g
Cholesterol 50mg
Total fat 5g
Saturated fat 2g
Sodium 240mg

250 g	lean lamb, minced	8 oz
4	courgettes, trimmed	4
1 tsp	virgin olive oil	1 tsp
½	garlic clove	½
30 g	sun-dried tomatoes, drained of any oil and chopped	1 oz
1 tbsp	tomato paste	1 tbsp
½ tsp	ground cinnamon	½ tsp
30 g	raisins	1 oz
15 g	pine nuts	½ oz
1½ tsp	balsamic vinegar	1½ tsp
2 tbsp	finely chopped fresh basil	2 tbsp
½ tsp	salt	½ tsp
¼ tsp	freshly ground black pepper	¼ tsp

Halve the courgettes lengthwise and arrange them in a single layer in a shallow dish, cut side upwards. Add 1 tablespoon of water and cover the dish with plastic film, pulling back one corner. Microwave the courgettes on high for 8 minutes; half way through the cooking time, rearrange them and move the inside pieces to the edge of the dish. Drain the courgettes. Scoop out the pulp, leaving the skins intact, and place in a sieve to drain.

Put the oil into a shallow dish and heat it on high for 15 seconds. Spear the garlic on a fork and wipe it round the hot dish to infuse the oil. Discard the garlic. Break up the minced lamb with a fork and add it to the dish, together with the sun-dried tomato, tomato paste and cinnamon. Cook on high until no pink meat is visible—3 to 4 minutes— breaking up the meat thoroughly with a fork after every minute. Drain off any fat.

Add the courgette pulp, raisins and pine-nuts to the meat, and stir in the vinegar, basil, salt and pepper. Pile the mixture into the courgette skins and arrange them in a singe layer in the shallow dish. Cover the dish with plastic film, leaving one corner open. Cook the stuffed courgettes on high until they are tender—4 to 6 minutes, rearranging them half way through the cooking time. Leave the to stand, covered, for 2 minutes before serving.

Bacon and Onion Potato Salad

Serves 6 as a side dish

Working time: about 10 minutes

Total time: about 20 minutes

Calories 140

Protein 3g

Cholesterol 2mg

Total fat 2g

Saturated fat 0g

Sodium 45mg

1 kg	small round red potatoes of equal size, scrubbed	**2 lb**
2	rashers bacon, cut into thin strips	**2**
1	red onion, thinly sliced	**1**
4 tbsp	finely chopped celery	**4 tbsp**
1 tbsp	cornflour, mixed with 12.5 cl (4 fl oz) unsalted chicken stock	**1 tbsp**
4 tbsp	white vinegar	**4 tbsp**
	freshly ground black pepper	
2 tbsp	coarsely chopped parsley	**2 tbsp**

Prick the potatoes with a fork in two places; any more punctures would let too much moisture escape.

Arrange them in a circle on absorbent paper towel in the microwave oven; cook them on high for 7 minutes. Turn the potatoes over and rearrange them; continue cooking them on high until they are barely soft—5 to 7 minutes more. Remove the potatoes from the oven and set them aside until they are cool enough to handle.

Put the bacon strips in a bowl; cover the bowl with a paper towel and microwave the bacon on high for 2 minutes. Remove the towel and drain off the excess fat, then add the onion and celery to the bowl. Toss the bacon and vegetables together, cover the bowl, and microwave on high for 90 seconds. Stir in the cornflour mixture and the vinegar. Cover the bowl and microwave it on high until the dressing thickens slightly—about 2 minutes.

Cut the potatoes into slices about 5 mm ($\frac{1}{4}$ inch) thick. Pour the dressing over the potato slices; add a generous grinding of pepper and half the parsley. Gently toss the salad, then cool. Scatter the remaining parsley over the top just before serving.

Toasted Turkey—Provolone Sandwiches with Jam

Serves 6 as
a main dish

Working
(and total)
time: about
45 minutes

Calories
445

Protein
31g

Cholesterol
60mg

Total fat
12g

Saturated fat
6g

Sodium
580mg

12	slices white sandwich bread	**12**
2 tsp	Dijon mustard	**2 tsp**
350 g	roast turkey breast meat, sliced	**12 oz**
175 g	provolone cheese, sliced	**6 oz**
1	large red onion, thinly sliced	**1**
12.5 cl	semi-skimmed milk	**4 fl oz**
1	egg white	**1**
¼ tsp	ground white pepper	**¼ tsp**

	Strawberry-cranberry jam	
100 g	fresh or frozen cranberries	**3½ oz**
1	orange, rind julienned, juice reserved	**1**
1	lemon, rind julienned, juice reserved	**1**
100 g	sugar	**3½ oz**
175 g	fresh strawberries, halved	**6 oz**

To make the jam, combine the cranberries, orange rind and juice, lemon rind and juice, and sugar in a saucepan. Bring the mixture to the boil, reduce the heat, and simmer the fruit for 5 minutes. Add the strawberries to the saucepan, stir well, and cook for an additional 5 minutes. Transfer the jam to a bowl and chill it.

Preheat the oven to 180°C (350°F or Mark 4).

Lay six of the bread slices out on a work surface and brush with the mustard. Divide the turkey, provolone cheese and onion am ng these six slices. Set the remaining of bread on top.

In a small bowl, whisk together the milk, egg white and pepper. Brush both sides of the sandwiches with this mixture. Heat a large griddle or frying pan over medium heat until a few drops of cold water dance when sprinkled on the surface. Put the sandwiches on the griddle or in the pan and cook them until the undersides are well browned—about 5 minutes. Turn the sandwiches and cook them until the second sides are browned—2 to 3 minutes more. Serve the sandwiches immediately, accompanied by the jam.

Aromatic Chicken Kofta

Makes 30 kofta

Working time: about 45 minutes

Total time: about 1 hour

Per kofta:

Calories 20

Protein 2g

Cholesterol 5mg

Total fat 1g

Saturated fat trace

Sodium 30mg

60 g	burghul	**2 oz**
12	cardamom pods, seeds only	**12**
250 g	boneless chicken breast, skinned and chopped	**8 oz**
1 tsp	ground coriander	**1 tsp**
½ tsp	ground cumin	**½ tsp**
45 g	mint, finely chopped	**1½ oz**
1	garlic clove, crushed	**1**
½ tsp	salt	**½ tsp**
	freshly ground black pepper	
2 tsp	virgin olive oil	**2 tsp**
	lemon and lime wedges, for garnish	

Put the burghul in a small saucepan and add water to cover the burghul by about 1 cm (½ inch). Bring to the boil, then cover the pan and simmer until the burghul is soft and all the water has been absorbed—about 15 minutes. Set aside to cool.

Set a heavy frying pan over high heat, add the cardamom seeds and cook until they start to pop—about 1 minute. Finely grind the seeds, using a rolling pin.

Preheat the grill to high. In a food processor, combine the chicken, ground cardamom seeds, coriander, cumin, mint, garlic, salt and a little pepper for a few seconds to form a paste. Add the chicken paste to the burghul and mix together, then roll the mixture into 30 small balls. Brush the balls with the oil, and cook under the grill until they are crisp and golden, turning frequently — 4 to 5 minutes. Serve the kofta hot, accompanied by the lemon and lime wedges.

Anchovy Toasts

Makes 16
toasts

Working time:
about 15
minutes

Total time:
about 40
minutes

Per toast:
Calories
50
Protein
1g
Cholesterol
5mg
Total fat
4g
Saturated fat
1g
Sodium
180mg

4	thin slices bread	4
45 g	small anchovy fillets, rinsed and drained	**1½ oz**
60 g	polyunsaturated margarine	**2 oz**
½ tsp	fresh lemon juice	**½ tsp**

⅛ tsp	cayenne pepper	**⅛ tsp**
	freshly ground black pepper	
	parsley or lemon wedges, for garnish (optional)	

Preheat the oven to 180°C (350°F or Mark 4). Cut out a diamond-shaped piece of cardboard with sides 5 cm (2 inches) long, and use this template to cut 16 diamonds from the slices of bread. Place the bread diamonds on a baking sheet in the oven and bake them until golden on both sides—about 25 minutes. Set aside.

Reserve four whole anchovy fillets, and pound the rest in a mortar until a smooth paste is obtained. Gradually beat in the margarine and season with the lemon juice, cayenne pepper and some black pepper.

Spread the anchovy mixture evenly on to the diamond toasts, then draw the tines of a fork through the mixture to produce decorative lines. Cut each of the reserved anchovies into four long, thin strips. Twist each strip and lay it on top of a toast. Serve garnished, if you like, with parsley or lemon wedges.

Baguette with Hot Prawn and Garlic Filling

Serves 6

Working time:
about 10
minutes

Total time:
about 20
minutes

Calories
165
Protein
10g
Cholesterol
40mg
Total fat
5g
Saturated fat
trace
Sodium
340mg

90 g	medium-fat curd cheese	**3 oz**	
½	garlic clove, crushed	**½**	
2 tsp	finely chopped fresh herbs such as parsley, chives and dill	**2 tsp**	
1 tsp	fresh lemon juice	**1 tsp**	
	freshly ground black pepper		
175 g	cooked peeled prawns, chopped	**6 oz**	
1	baguette, about 60 cm (2 feet) long or six crusty rolls	**1**	

Preheat the oven to 220°C (425°F or Mark 7).

In a medium-sized bowl, mix together the curd cheese, garlic, herbs, lemon juice and some black pepper. Stir in the prawns.

Cut deep diagonal slashes at 4 cm (1½ inch) intervals in the baguette, taking care not to slice right through. Stuff the slashes with the prawn mixture.

Wrap the baguette loosely in foil and bake in the oven for 10 minutes. Serve hot.

Tomato and Prosciutto Toasts

Serves 8

Working (and total) time: 20 minutes

Calories 270
Protein 11g
Cholesterol 5mg
Total fat 7g
Saturated fat 1g
Sodium 200mg

4	long crusty bread rolls	4	1 tsp	chopped fresh marjoram	1 tsp
2	tomatoes, skinned and finely chopped	2	½ tsp	salt freshly ground black pepper	½ tsp
2	garlic cloves, crushed	2	100 g	thinly sliced prosciutto trimmed of fat	3½ oz
2 tbsp	virgin olive oil	2 tbsp			

Cut the rolls in half and toast on the cut side.

Mix together the chopped tomatoes, garlic, olive oil, marjoram, salt and some freshly ground black pepper. Divide the tomato mixture among the toasted rolls, spread it evenly and press well into the surface.

Cut the prosciutto into strips and arrange a few strips over the top of each roll.

Serve the tomato and prosciutto toasts immediately, while the bread is still warm.

Savoury Filled Loaf

Serves 6

Working time
about 25
minutes

Total time:
about 1 hour

Calories
80
Protein
4g
Cholesterol
5mg
Total fat
3g
Saturated fat
1g
Sodium
350mg

175 g	button mushrooms, quartered	6 oz
1 tbsp	safflower oil	1 tbsp
1½ tbsp	fresh lemon juice	1½ tbsp
2 tsp	fresh thyme, or ½ tsp dried thyme	2 tsp
½ tsp	salt	½ tsp

	freshly ground black pepper	
1	small white cob loaf, about 15 cm (6 inches) in diameter	1
60 g	thinly sliced prosciutto	2 oz
3	tomatoes, skinned, seeded and thinly sliced	3

In a small, heavy frying pan, sauté the mushrooms in the oil and lemon juice until their juices run. Stir in the thyme, salt and a little pepper, then set aside. Preheat the oven to 190°C (375°F or Mark 5).

Slice off the top of the loaf to form a lid about 2.5 cm (1 inch) thick at its centre. With your fingers, scoop out bread from the centre of the loaf, leaving a 1 cm (½ inch) thick base and sides; use the scooped-out bread to make breadcrumbs for another dish.

Arrange the mushrooms in the bottom of the breadcase. Lay the slices of prosciutto on top of the mushrooms; the ends of the slices should overhang the sides of the loaf. Arrange the tomatoes on top of the prosciutto, add a little pepper, then fold over the overhanging ham to enclose the tomatoes. Replace the lid. Loosely wrap the loaf in foil and bake for 30 minutes.

Unwrap the loaf from the foil, cut it into wedges and serve warm.

Creamed Mushrooms on Toast

Serves 2

Working (and total) time: about 15 minutes

Calories 150
Protein 5g
Cholesterol 10mg
Total fat 5g
Saturated fat 2g
Sodium 400mg

2	slices granary bread	**2**
15 cl	unsalted chicken stock	**¼ pint**
1 tbsp	Madeira	**1 tbsp**
1 tsp	fresh lemon juice	**1 tsp**
175 g	button mushrooms, wiped clean	**6 oz**

2 tbsp	crème fraîche	**2 tbsp**
¼ tsp	salt	**¼ tsp**
	freshly ground black pepper	
½ tsp	Dijon mustard	**½ tsp**
½ tsp	mustard seeds	**½ tsp**

Toast the slices of bread on one side only and set aside.

Pour the stock, Madeira and lemon juice into a shallow, lidded saucepan and bring to the boil. Reduce the heat, add the mushrooms and simmer for about 4 minutes. Remove the mushrooms and set aside.

To reduce the cooking liquid, place the saucepan over high heat and boil until about 2 tablespoons of liquid remain. Add the crème fraîche and reduce further for a few seconds. Return the mushrooms to the liquid, warm through, and season with the salt, some pepper and the mustard.

Pour the mixture on to the untoasted side of the bread, sprinkle with the mustard seeds and place under a hot grill for about 20 seconds, until the seeds pop. Serve at once.

Chicken and Orange Pittas

Serves 6

Working (and total) time: about 15 minutes

Calories
180

Protein
18g

Cholesterol
5mg

Total fat
7g

Saturated fat
1g

Sodium
230mg

2	oranges	**2**
350 g	cooked chicken breast, diced	**12 oz**
½	small crisp lettuce, leaves torn into small pieces	**½**
3	wholemeal pittas	**3**

Watercress dressing		
90 g	watercress, stems removed	**3 oz**
2 tbsp	mayonnaise	**2 tbsp**
2 tbsp	plain low-fat yogurt	**2 tbsp**
¼ tsp	salt	**¼ tsp**
	freshly ground black pepper	

Preheat the oven to 200°C (400°F or Mark 6). Put all the ingredients for the dressing in a blender or food processor and purée for a few seconds until smooth. Set the dressing aside.

Cut away the peel, white pith and outer membrane from the oranges. To separate the orange segments from the inner membranes, slice down to the core with a sharp knife on either side of each segment; cut each segment in half. Place the chicken, lettuce and orange segments in a bowl and mix together.

Warm the pittas in the oven until they puff up — about 1 minute. Cut them in half, then open up each half to form a pocket; stuff the pittas with the chicken mixture. Spoon generous amounts of watercress dressing into each pitta half and serve immediately.

Seafood and Asparagus Muffins

Serves 4

Working
(and total)
time: about
30 minutes

Calories
180
Protein
15g
Cholesterol
50mg
Total fat
8g
Saturated fat
4g
Sodium
365mg

4	asparagus spears, trimmed	**4**
16	fresh mussels, scrubbed and debearded	**16**
30 g	unsalted butter, softened	**1 oz**

2 tsp	tomato paste	**2 tsp**
1 tbsp	finely chopped fresh dill	**1 tbsp**
2	wholemeal muffins or baps	**2**
125 g	peeled, cooked prawns	**4 oz**

Cook the asparagus in a saucepan of boiling water until tender—5 to 6 minutes—then drain in a colander and refresh under cold running water. Drain well. Cut off the tips, leaving them whole, and slice the stalks. Set the asparagus aside.

Pour 4 tablespoons of water into a large saucepan. Add the mussels, cover the pan and bring the water to the boil. Steam the mussels until their shells open—4 to 5 minutes. Let the mussels cool in their liquid, then remove them from the pan, discarding any that remain closed. Using the edge of a spoon, detach the flesh from the shells. Set the mussels aside and discard the shells.

In a small bowl, mix together the butter, tomato paste and dill, blending them well. Split the muffins in half and toast them under a hot grill for 1 to 2 minutes each side until they are lightly browned.

Spread the muffin halves thinly with about half of the tomato butter, then divide the mussels, prawns, and asparagus slices and tips among the muffins. Melt the remaining tomato butter and brush it over the top of the seafood and asparagus.

Place the muffins under a medium grill for 3 to 4 minutes, to heat them through, and serve immediately.

Calzone

Makes 10
calzone

Working time:
about 40
minutes

Total: time:
about 2 hours
(includes
proving)

Per calzone:

Calories
225

Protein
11g

Cholesterol
15mg

Total fat
6g

Saturated fat
3g

Sodium
400mg

500 g	plain flour, sifted	1 lb
1½ tsp	salt	1½ tsp
15 g	fresh yeast	½ oz
1 tbsp	virgin olive	1 tbsp
500 g	large tomatoes, chopped	1 lb

1 tbsp	tomato paste	1 tbsp
1 tsp	dried oregano	1 tsp
	freshly ground black pepper	
175 g	low-fat mozzarella cheese, sliced	6 oz
60 g	prosciutto, chopped	2 oz

Cream the fresh yeast with 15 cl (½ pint) of water and leave for 10 to 15 minutes, until frothy. Sift the flour and salt into a large bowl and make a well in the centre. Pour in the yeast mixture and mix in enough tepid water to make a soft but firm dough. Turn the dough on to a floured surface and knead until it is smooth and elastic—about 10 minutes. Return the dough to the bowl, cover with plastic film and leave to rise in a warm place until doubled in size—about 1 hour.

To make the filling, heat the oil in a small pan over medium heat, add the tomatoes and tomato paste, and cook for about 5 minutes. Stir in the oregano, the remaining salt and some pepper, then leave to cool. Preheat the oven to 220°C (425°F or Mark 7).

Turn the dough on to a floured surface, knead for a few minutes, then divide it into 10 pieces. Roll out each piece into a rectangle approximately 20 by 10 cm (8 by 4 inches). Spread the tomato mixture over one half of each rectangle, leaving a small border. Reserve any tomato juices in the pan. Top the tomato mixture with the mozzarella and prosciutto, then dampen the edges of the dough, fold the dough over the filling, and press the edges together to seal them. Arrange the calzone on a lightly oiled baking sheet and brush them with the reserved tomato juices. Cover with plastic film and leave to rise for 10 minutes.

Bake the calzone in the oven until they are golden—8 to 10 minutes. Serve hot.

Goat Cheese on Toast

Serves 4

Working time: about 30 minutes

Total time: about 12 hours and 40 minutes

Calories 180

Protein 8g

Cholesterol 20mg

Total fat 11g

Saturated fat 4g

Sodium 370mg

2	small goat cheeses, about 100 g ($3\frac{1}{2}$ oz) total weight	2
2 tbsp	virgin olive oil	**2 tbsp**
$\frac{1}{2}$ tsp	crushed black peppercorns	**$\frac{1}{2}$ tsp**
1	bay leaf	**1**
1	garlic clove, crushed	**1**
1 tbsp	finely chopped fresh herbs, such as chives, tarragon or rosemary	**1 tbsp**
4	thin slices French bread, cut diagonally	**4**
30 g	fresh breadcrumbs	**1 oz**
125 g	assorted salad leaves	**4 oz**

Remove the thin layer of rind on the cheeses and cut each cheese into four rounds. Mix the oil, peppercorns, bay leaf, garlic and herbs in a bowl, and add the cheese rounds. Turn them so that they are well coated, then leave them to marinate in the refrigerator for about 12 hours.

Preheat the oven to 180°C (350°F or Mark 4). Put the bread slices in the oven for about 4 minutes, then brush them with the marinade.

Meanwhile, increase the temperature to 240°C (475°F or Mark 9).

Remove the cheese slices from the marinade and dip them in the breadcrumbs, pressing lightly to make the crumbs adhere. Place two cheese slices on each toast and return to the oven until the toast is slightly brown and the cheese softened — about 10 minutes. Serve the hot toasts surrounded by the salad leaves.

Aubergines Stuffed with Lamb and Buckwheat

Serves 4

Working (and total) time: about 40 minutes

Calories
200
Protein
13g
Cholesterol
30mg
Total fat
11g
Saturated fat
2g
Sodium
140mg

30 g	roasted buckwheat groats (kasha)	**1 oz**
2	aubergines, stalks left on, pierced	**2**
1	small onion, finely chopped	**1**
1 tbsp	safflower oil	**1 tbsp**
30 g	pine-nuts, finely chopped	**1 oz**
150 g	cooked lean lamb, minced	**5 oz**

3 tsp	chopped fresh oregano	**3 tsp**
2 tsp	sweet paprika	**2 tsp**
¼ tsp	salt	**¹/₄ tsp**
4	medium tomatoes, puréed	**4**
1 tbsp	chopped parsley	**1 tbsp**
	freshly ground black pepper	

Place the buckwheat groats in a bowl and microwave on high for 30 seconds. Add 12 .5 cl (4 fl oz) of hot water and microwave on high until it is nearly absorbed—about 4 minutes more. Cover with plastic film and set aside.

Arrange the aubergines in a deep baking dish and add 4 tablespoons of water. Cover with plastic film, leaving a corner open. Microwave on high until they are soft and their colour fades—about 10 minutes.

Meanwhile, prepare the stuffing. Put the onion in a glass bowl with the oil and microwave on high until soft—about 3 to 4 minutes. Stir in the pine-nuts and microwave on high for 1 minute, stir again and microwave on high until the nuts begin to

brown—about 30 seconds. Stir in the lamb, oregano, buckwheat, paprika, salt and 2 tablespoons of the pureed tomato.

Halve the aubergines lengthwise. With a spoon, scoop out most of the flesh from each half, leaving a shell. Chop the flesh, stir it into the lamb and buckwheat, and pile this stuffing into the aubergine shells. Arrange the shells on a platter, leaving a space in the centre for a small bowl. Cover with parchment paper and microwave on high until hot—about 4 minutes. Sprinkle with the parsley.

Season the remaining puréed tomato with plenty of pepper. Put the purée in a bowl and microwave on high for 1 minute. Place this in the centre of the aubergines and serve.

Brill and Leek Croustades

Serves 4
Working and total time about 50 minutes

Calories 200
Protein 10g
Cholesterol 10mg
Total fat 8g
Saturated fat 1g
Sodium 300mg

½	day-old loaf white bread, crust removed	½	125 g	skinned brill fillets, cut into strips	4 oz
1 tbsp	safflower oil	1 tbsp	½ litre	unsalted fish stock	16 fl oz
125 g	leeks, trimmed and cubed	4 oz	60 g	fromage frais	2 oz
12.5 cl	medium dry white wine	4 fl oz	1 tbsp	finely cut chives	1 tbsp

Preheat the oven to 170°C or Mark 3)

Cut the bread into four 4 cm (1½ inch) thick slices, about 7.5 cm (3 inches) square. Cut a square from the top of each slice, 5 mm (¼ inch) in from each edge and within 5 mm (¼ inch) of the base. Carefully hollow out this shape, leaving a croustade case. Brush the cases lightly with oil and bake until crisp and golden—about 40 minutes. Meanwhile, prepare the filling.

In a saucepan. simmer the leeks in the wine until they are tender and the wine is almost completely evaporated. Place the strips of brill on top of the leeks, pour in the stock, which should just cover the fish, reduce the heat so that the liqiud barely moves in the pan and poach the fish for 30 seconds

Remove the fish from the stock and place it in a dish. Transfer the leeks in the same way to a separated heated dish, and cover to keep warm. Boil the stock until it is reduced to 4 tablespoons. Reduce the heat to very low and stir in the *fromage frais*. Lightly fold the brill into the sauce and gently heat hrough — being careful not to boil.

Place a quarter of the leeks in each croustade. Spoon on the brill, sprinkle with the chives and serve.

Chicken, Celery and Pistachio Nut Baps

Makes 6 filled baps

Working (and total) time: about 25 minutes

Per filled bap:
Calories
200
Protein
15g
Cholesterol
20mg
Total fat
4g
Saturated fat
1g
Sodium
360mg

6	wholemeal baps	6
6 tbsp	low-fat fromage frais	6 tbsp
175 g	skinned cooked chicken breast, cut into strips	6 oz
1 tbsp	wholegrain mustard	1 tbsp
6	iceberg lettuce leaves	6
2	small sticks celery, trimmed and thinly sliced	2
18	skinned shelled pistachio nuts, finely sliced	18
	cayenne pepper, for garnish	

Cut the baps in half and spread each bottom half evenly with 1 tablespoon of the *fromage frais*. Spread the mustard over the chicken breast strips.

Place a lettuce leaf on top of each covered base and divide the chicken strips, celery slices and pistachio nuts among them. Garnish each filling with a light dusting of cayenne pepper and replace the top halves of the baps.

Chilled Turkey with Creamy Tuna Sauce

Serves 6

Working time:
about 30
minutes

Total time:
about 40
minutes

Calories
285
Protein
31g
Cholesterol
70mg
Total fat
15g
Saturated fat
2g
Sodium
125mg

750 g	boneless turkey breast meat skinned and cubed	**1½ lb**
½ tsp	virgin olive oil	**½ tsp**
½ tsp	safflower oil	**½ tsp**
⅛ tsp	salt	**⅛ tsp**
12.5 cl	unsalted turkey or chicken stock, warmed	**4 fl oz**
	fresh sage, finely sliced	

	Tuna sauce	
100 g	can tuna, packed in brine, drained	**3½ oz**
3 tbsp	virgin olive oil	**3 tbsp**
2 tbsp	safflower oil	**2 tbsp**
5 tbsp	buttermilk	**5 tbsp**
1 tsp	fresh lime juice	**1 tsp**
1 tsp	capers, rinsed and patted dry	**1 tsp**

Heat the oils in a large, heavy frying pan over medium heat. Sauté the turkey pieces for 3 minutes and turn them over. Sprinkle with the salt and cook for another 3 minutes. Add the stock, lower the heat, and simmer for 2 minutes more. Remove each piece as it whitens. Set aside to cool. Reduce the stock to about 4 tablespoons and reserve for the sauce.

To make the sauce, purée the tuna with the stock in a food processor or a blender. Scrape down the sides with a rubber spatula and

process another 10 seconds With the motor still running, pour in the oils slowly. Add the buttermilk, lime juice and capers, and process for 1 minute more or until smooth. (Alternatively, pound the tuna to a paste in a mortar.) Transfer the sauce to a bowl and refrigerate.

To assemble the dish, pour a little sauce on individual plates. Put a portion of the turkey on each plate and dribble the remaining sauce over the turkey. Garnish with sage or with chopped parsley.

Greek-Style Chicken and Rice Casserole

Serves 8 as a main dish

Total time about 1 hour

Calories 275

Protein 17g

Cholesterol 50mg

Total fat 11g

Saturated fat 3g

Sodium 245mg

2 tbsp	safflower oil	2 tbsp
8	chicken thighs, skinned	8
175 g	long-grain rice	6 oz
1	onion, chopped	1
4	garlic cloves, finely chopped	4
¼ litre	unsalted chicken stock	8 fl oz
800 g	canned whole tomatoes	1¾ lb
3 tbsp	chopped fresh oregano	3 tbsp
1 tbsp	fresh thyme	1 tbsp
12	oil-cured olives, stoned and quartered, or 12 stoned black olives, coarsely chopped	12
30 g	feta cheese, rinsed and crumbled	1 oz

Heat the oil in a large, heavy fireproof casserole over medium-high heat. Add four of the thighs and cook them until they are lightly browned—about 4 minutes on each side. Remove the first four thighs and brown the other four. Set all the thighs aside.

Reduce the heat to medium and add the rice, onion, garlic and 4 tablespoons of the stock. Cook the mixture, stirring constantly, until the onion is translucent—about 4 minutes. Add the remaining stock, the tomatoes, the oregano and the thyme. Push the thighs down into the rice mixture. Bring the liquid to the boil, reduce the heat, and simmer the chicken, tightly covered, until the rice is tender—20 to 30 minutes.

Stir the olives into the chicken and rice, and serve with the feta cheese on top.

Lamb Loaf Stuffed with Dried Apricots

Serves 6

Working time:
about 1 hour

Total time:
about 2 hours

Calories
290
Protein
27g
Cholesterol
80mg
Total fat
10g
Saturated fat
3g
Sodium
270mg

500 g	lean lamb, trimmed and minced	**1 lb**		**1 tbsp**	finely chopped sultanas	**1 tbsp**
100 g	spllt red lentils	**3½ oz**		**1 tbsp**	fresh lemon juice	**1 tbsp**
4 tbsp	finely cut fresh dill	**4 tbsp**		**1 tbsp**	safflower oil	**1 tbsp**
2 tbsp	grated onion	**2 tbsp**		**1**	large onion, finely chopped	**1**
3	garlic cloves, crushed	**3**		**20 cl**	unsalted brown or	**7 fl oz**
2 tsp	ground tumeric	**2 tsp**			chicken stock	
¼ tsp	freshly grated nutmeg	**¼ tsp**			**Dill sauce**	
1	large egg white, lightly beaten	**1**		**6 tbsp**	thick Greek yogurt	**6 tbsp**
½ tsp	salt	**½ tsp**		**4 tbsp**	plain low-fat yogurt	**4 tbsp**
	freshly ground black pepper			**2 tbsp**	finely cut fresh dill	**2 tbsp**
100 g	dried apricots, finely chopped	**3½ oz**		**⅛ tsp**	salt	**⅛ tsp**
2 tbsp	sunflower seeds	**2 tbsp**			freshly ground black pepper	

Cook the lentils in boiling water for 20 minutes, drain and put in a bowl. Add the minced lamb, the dill, grated onion, garlic, turmeric, nutmeg, egg white, salt and some black pepper. Knead well to combine.

Mix together the dried apricots, sunflower seeds, sultanas and lemon juice in a separate bowl. Divide the meat mixture in two and flatten each half into an oval about 2 cm (¾ inch) thick. Shape the stuffing into two smaller ovals

and place in the centre of the ovals of meat. Fold over to make loaves and fry them until they are lightly browned—about 5 minutes.

Wipe the pan clean and brown the onion. Stir in the stock and bring it to the boil, then lower the heat and add the meat loaves. Cover and simmer for 45 minutes to 1 hour.

Combine the Greek and plain yogurt, stir in the dill and season with the salt and pepper.

Slice the loaf and serve with the sauce.

Mushrooms and Asparagus in Phyllo Cases

Serves 6

Working
(and total)
time: about
1 hour

Calories
105
Protein
5g
Cholesterol
0mg
Total fat
4g
Saturated fat
1g
Sodium
90mg

4 tsp	safflower oil	4 tsp	350 g	button mushrooms, sliced	12 oz
6	sheets phyllo pastry, each about 45 by 30 cm (18 by 12 inches)	6	¼ litre	skimmed milk	8 fl oz
			2 tsp	cornflour	2 tsp
250 g	asparagus, trimmed and peeled	8 oz	1 tbsp	chopped fresh tarragon	1 tbsp
2	carrots, julienned, parboiled for 5 minutes and drained	2	1 tsp	fresh lemon juice	1 tsp
4	large spring onions, sliced	4	⅛ tsp	salt	⅛ tsp
1	garlic clove, crushed	1		freshly ground black pepper	

Preheat the oven to 190°C (375°F or Mark 5). Brush the bases of six 15 cl (¼ pint) ramekins with 2 teaspoons of oil.

Fold each sheet of phyllo pastry in half lengthwise, then in three crosswise, to make six 15 cm (6 inch) squares. Trim the edges to give six stacks of pastry each containing six squares. Rearrange each stack to resemble the petals of a flower. Place a stack of squares in each ramekin and bake in the oven for 15 to 20 minutes, until the cases are browned.

Steam the asparagus over a pan of gently simmering water until tender. Reserve twelve tips for garnish. Chop the remaining asparagus.

With the remaining 2 teaspoons of oil, fry the spring onions, garlic and mushrooms. Cook until the mushrooms begin to exude their juices. Add the milk and bring the mixture to the boil. Blend the cornflour to a paste with 2 tablespoons of water. Add this to the sauce and simmer to thicken it. Gently mix in the chopped tarragon, lemon juice, chopped asparagus, carrots, salt and some black pepper. Simmer for 1 minute more.

Remove the phyllo cases from the ramekins, and spoon on the vegetable mixture. Garnish with the reserved asparagus and a sprig of tarragon.

Orzo and Mussels

Serves 4

Working time: about 30 minutes

Total time: about 40 minutes

Calories 400
Protein 17g
Cholesterol 20mg
Total fat 9g
Saturated fat 1g
Sodium 390mg

250 g	orzo	8 oz
1	orange	1
2 tbsp	virgin olive oil	2 tbsp
1	onion, finely chopped	1
4	garlic cloves, finely chopped	4
1 kg	tomatoes, skinned, seeded and finely chopped	2 lb
2 tsp	fennel seeds	2 tsp
1½ tbsp	tomato paste	1½ tbsp
12.5 cl	dry vermouth	4 fl oz
¼ tsp	salt	¼ tsp
3 tbsp	chopped fresh parsley	3 tbsp
1 tsp	fresh thyme	1 tsp
750 g	mussels, scrubbed and debearded	1½ lb

Pare the rind from the orange and cut it into tiny julienne. Put the strips in a small saucepan with ¼ litre (8 fl oz) of water. Bring the water to the boil, then remove the pan from the heat. Rinse the rind and set it aside. Squeeze the juice from the orange and reserve it as well.

Heat the oil in a casserole over medium heat. Add the chopped onion and cook it for 3 minutes, stirring constantly Add the chopped garlic and cook, stirring, until the onion is translucent—about 2 minutes more.

Push the onion-garlic mixture to one side of the casserole. Add the tomatoes and the fennel seeds, and raise the heat. Cook the

tomatoes just enough to soften them—1 minute. Stir the onion-garlic mixture in with the tomatoes. Add the tomato paste, orange juice, vermouth and salt to the casserole, and stir well. Reduce the heat and simmer for 5 minutes. Add the parsley, thyme and orange rind.

Place the mussels on top of the sauce. Cover and steam until the mussels open—3 to 5 minutes. Discard any that remain closed. Set the casserole aside, keeping it warm.

Add the orzo to 3 litres (5 pints) of boiling water with 1½ teaspoons of salt. Cook it until it is *al dente*. Drain and divide it between four plates. Ladle on the mussels and sauce.

Oyster Mushroom Ramekins

Serves 4

Working time: about 20 minutes

Total time: about 35 minutes

Calories
45
Protein
3g
Cholesterol
55mg
Total fat
3g
Saturated fat
1g
Sodium
75mg

1 tsp	safflower oil	**1 tsp**
1	small onion, finely chopped	**1**
2 tsp	chopped fresh chervil	**2 tsp**
250 g	oyster mushrooms, finely chopped	**8 oz**
1	egg, separated, plus one egg white	**1**

1 tbsp	double cream	**1 tbsp**
⅛ tsp	salt	**⅛ tsp**
	freshly ground black pepper	
	fresh chervil sprigs, for garnish	

Preheat the oven to 180°C (350°F or Mark 4).

In a heavy-bottomed saucepan, heat the oil. Add the onion, and sauté until soft—about 3 minutes. Stir the chopped chervil into the onion then, using a slotted spoon, transfer the mixture to a bowl and set aside.

In the same pan, sauté the mushrooms for 2 minutes. Remove about two thirds of the mushrooms from the pan with a slotted spoon and combine them with the onion and the chervil. Divide the mixture among four 12.5 cl (4fl oz) ramekins.

Drain the remaining mushrooms; reserve

their cooking juices for another use. Put the mushrooms in a bowl with the egg yolk and cream and stir well.

In a clean bowl, whisk the egg whites until they are stiff. Fold them gently into the egg yolk and mushroom mixture. Season the mixture with the salt and some pepper and spoon it into the ramekins.

Bake the ramekins in the oven until the fillings are puffed up, firm to the touch and lightly browned—about 15 minutes Serve the soufflés immediately, garnished with the fresh chervil sprigs.

Skewered Sardines with Watercress Sauce

Serves 4

Working time: about 50 minutes

Total time: about 1 hour and 50 minutes

Calories 420
Protein 35g
Cholesterol 90mg
Total fat 25g
Saturated fat 7g
Sodium 230mg

8	large sardines	8
½ tsp	cayenne pepper	½ tsp
24	black peppercorns, crushed	24
1 tbsp	virgin olive oil	1 tbsp
½ tsp	salt	½ tsp
1	lime, rind only, finely grated	1
	watercress sprigs for garnish	

	lemon wedges (optional)	
	Watercress sauce	
30 cl	fish stock	½ pint
125 g	watercress, trimmed	4 oz
15 g	unsalted butter	½ oz
15 g	flour	½ oz
1 tbsp	double cream	1 tbsp

Remove the fins, scales and viscera, but not the heads, from the sardines. Wash the fish and dry well.

Put the cayenne pepper, peppercorns, oil, salt and grated lime rind in a large, shallow dish and mix them together. Place the sardines in the marinade, turning them until evenly coated. Cover and marinate for 1 hour.

Pour the fish stock into a small saucepan and bring to the boil. Add the watercress and cook for 10 minutes, until softened, then purée in a food blender for 1 minute.

Melt the butter in the pan, stir in the flour, then the puréed watercress. Bring to the boil, stirring all the time. Reduce the heat and simmer the sauce for 10 to 15 minutes.

Meanwhile, remove the sardines from the marinade and thread them on to wooden or metal skewers. Cook under a hot grill for 4 to 5 minutes, turning them once during cooking.

Stir the cream into the sauce then pour into a jug. Serve the sardines garnished with watercress and, if liked, lemon wedges. Hand the sauce separately.

Prosciutto, Mange-Tout and Tomato Croustades

Serves 4

Working (and total) time: about 1 hour

Calories 140
Protein 6g
Cholesterol 15 mg
Total fat 7g
Saturated fat 2g
Sodium 350mg

½	large day-old loaf white bread	½	
1 tbsp	safflower oil	1 tbsp	
5 tsp	dry sherry	5 tsp	
45 cl	unsalted chicken stock	¾ pint	
½ tsp	herb or Dijon mustard	½ tsp	
60 g	mange-tout strings removed, cut diagonally in half	2 oz	
175 g	ripe tomatoes, skinned, seeded and cubed	6 oz	
60 g	prosciutto, trimmed of all fat and finely shredded	2 oz	
7 g	unsalted butter, chilled and cut into cubes	¼ oz	

Preheat the oven to 170°C or Mark 3)

Trim the crust from the bread and cut it into four 4 cm (1½ inch) thick slices, about 7.5 cm (3 inches) square. Cut a square from the top of each slice, 5 mm (¼ inch) in from each edge and within 5 mm (¼ inch) of the base. Carefully hollow out this shape, leaving a croustade case. Brush the cases lightly with oil and bake until crisp and golden—about 40 minutes. Meanwhile, prepare the filling.

In a small pan, boil the sherry over high heat until reduced to about 2 teaspoons. Stir in the stock and boil the liquid until reduced to about 10 cl (3½ fl oz). Add the mustard, lower the heat and keep the liquid warm.

Steam the mange-tout for about 1½ minutes, then drain them in a colander. Reserve eight mange-tout for garnish and transfer the remainder to a bowl. Add the tomatoes and prosciutto, and toss them lightly.

Reduce the heat under the saucepan to very low, and swirl in the cold butter cubes to thicken the sauce. Remove from the heat.

Divide the mange-tout, prosciutto and tomato mixture among the four croustades, spoon the sauce over the croustades, and serve warm, garnished with the reserved mange-tout pieces.

Quick Fried Scallops

Serves 4

Working
(and total)
time: about
30 minutes

Calories
225
Protein
29g
Cholesterol
50mg
Total fat
9g
Saturated fat
1g
Sodium
450mg

2 tbsp	almond oil	**2 tbsp**	
1	bulb lemon grass, crushed	**1**	
2.5 cm	piece fresh ginger root, crushed	**1 inch**	
6	kumquats, sliced in rings	**6**	
2 tsp	rice vinegar	**2 tsp**	
¼ tsp	salt	**¼ tsp**	

	white pepper		
12	cos lettuce leaves,	**12**	
1 tbsp	mint leaves, torn into pieces	**1 tbsp**	
1 tbsp	fresh coriander leaves	**1 tbsp**	
500 g	shelled scallops, bright white connective tissue removed	**1 lb**	

In a heavy frying pan, gently warm 1 tablespoon of the almond oil. Remove the pan from the heat and place the lemon grass and the ginger in the oil to infuse it with their flavours for at least 5 minutes. Meanwhile, blanch the kumquat rings in boiling water until they are soft—about 5 minutes—and drain them. Strain the flavoured oil. Discard the ginger and lemon grass.

Combine the remaining tablespoon of almond oil, 1 teaspoon of the rice vinegar, a little of the salt and some pepper in a large bowl. Place the lettuce leaves in the bowl and toss them to coat with the dressing. Mix in the mint and the coriander leaves. Transfer the salad to four serving dishes.

Rinse the scallops under cold running water and pat them dry. Detach the corals and chop finely. Slice large scallops horizontally in three, leave smaller scallops whole.

In the frying pan, heat the flavoured oil until it is fairly hot. Toss the whites of the scallops in the oil, and cook them, stirring gently, for 1 minute. Lower the heat, add the kumquat rings, and cook gently for another minute. Stir in the chopped coral, cook the mixture for 30 seconds more and remove it from the heat. Sprinkle on the remaining rice vinegar and season lightly with the remaining salt and some pepper.

Arrange the scallops and kumquats on the four individual beds of salad. Serve warm.

Spiced Crab Puffs

Serves 4

Working time:
about 30
minutes

Total time:
about 55
minutes

Calories
245
Protein
10g
Cholesterol
80mg
Total fat
12g
Saturated fat
3g
Sodium
200mg

1 tbsp	safflower oil	**1 tbsp**
1	large garlic clove, finely chopped	**1**
1 tsp	grated fresh ginger root	**1 tsp**
3	spring onions, chopped	**3**
100 g	white crab meat, picked over and flaked	**3½ oz**
1 tbsp	rice vinegar	**1 tbsp**
1 tsp	soy sauce or shoyu	**1 tsp**
¼ tsp	hot red pepper flakes	**¼ tsp**
1 tbsp	chopped fresh coriander	**1 tbsp**
	Choux dough	
30 g	polyunsaturated margarine	**1 oz**
15 cl	skimmed milk	**¼ pint**
75 g	plain flour	**2½ oz**
¼ tsp	five-spice powder	**¼ tsp**
⅛ tsp	cayenne pepper	**⅛ tsp**
1	egg	**1**
1	egg white	**1**

Preheat the oven to 190°C (375°F or Mark 5). To make the choux dough, put the margarine and the milk in a saucepan. Cook gently until the margarine melts, then bring the liquid to the boil. Meanwhile, sift the flour, five-spice powder and cayenne pepper on to a sheet of greaseproof paper. Add this to the pan and stir until the mixture is well amalgamated. Remove the pan from the heat.

Lightly beat the egg with the egg white, then add it to the dough in the pan, beating it in a little at a time. Drop the dough in eight dollops on to a dampened baking sheet. Bake the pastries until they are risen and crisp—20 to 25 minutes. Make a slit in the side of each puff to allow steam to escape, then return the puffs to the oven to keep warm.

Heat the oil in a heavy frying pan over medium-high heat. Add the garlic and ginger, and stir-fry for 30 seconds. Add the spring onions and crab meat, and stir-fry for 1 minute. Stir in the vinegar, soy sauce and red pepper flakes, and cook for another 30 seconds. Remove from the heat and stir in the coriander. Spoon about a tablespoon of filling into each puff through the slit. Serve warm.

Turkey, Apple and Champagne Patties

Serves 10
as a main
dish

Working
(and total)
time:
about 45
minutes

Calories
110

Protein
14g

Cholesterol
30mg

Total fat
2g

Saturated fat
1g

Sodium
160mg

1	red apple, cored and chopped	1		500 g	turkey breast meat, minced	1 lb
1	onion, finely chopped	1		125 g	pork fillet. trimmed and minced	4 oz
90 g	fine dry breadcrumbs	3 oz		½ tsp	salt	½ tsp
12.5 cl	champagne or other sparkling dry white wine	4 fl oz			freshly ground black pepper	

Gently cook the apple and onion in a frying pan until they are soft—about 4 minutes.

Combine the breadcrumbs and the wine in a bowl. Add the turkey, pork, salt, some pepper and the apple-onion mixture, kneading the ingredients with your hands to mix them well. Shape the sausage meat into 20 patties about 1 cm (1 ½ inch) thick.

Heat a large, non-stick frying pan over medium heat and put half the patties into it. Cook them until the undersides are brown, then turn the patties over, and brown the other sides—about 4 minutes in all. Remove the browned patties to a platter and keep them warm while you cook the others. Serve the patties at once.

Chicken Parmesan

Serves 4

Working time:
about 15
minutes

Total time:
about 40
minutes

Calories
370
Protein
33g
Cholesterol
95mg
Total fat
17g
Saturated fat
5g
Sodium
695mg

8	chicken drumsticks, skinned, rinsed and patted dry	8
1	small onion, chopped	1
1	apple, peeled, cored and finely grated	1
1 tbsp	safflower oil	1 tbsp
35 cl	puréed tomatoes	12 fl oz
2 tbsp	tomato paste	2 tbsp
2 tbsp	Madeira	2 tbsp

1	garlic clove, finely chopped	1
1 tbsp	chopped fresh basil, or 1 tsp dried basil	1 tbsp
¼ tsp	dried oregano	¼ tsp
	freshly ground black pepper	
45 g	cornflakes, crushed	1½ oz
60 g	Parmesan cheese, freshly grated	2 oz
12.5 cl	plain low-fat yoghurt	4 fl oz

Combine the onion and apple with the oil in a bowl. Cover with a paper towel and microwave on high for 1 minute. Stir in the puréed tomatoes, tomato paste, Madeira, garlic, basil, oregano and some pepper. Cover the bowl with a paper towel again and microwave on medium (50 per cent power) for 9 minutes, stirring the sauce three times during the cooking. Remove the bowl from the oven and let it stand.

While the sauce is cooking, prepare the drumsticks. Sprinkle them with some pepper. Mix the cornflake crumbs and the Parmesan cheese. Dip the drumsticks into the yoghurt, then dredge them in the crumbcheese mixture, coating them evenly. Arrange the drumsticks on a microwave roasting rack with the meatier parts towards the outside of the rack. Microwave on high for 15 minutes, turning the dish once half way through the cooking time. Remove the drumsticks and let them stand for 7 minutes; then arrange them on a serving platter. Reheat the sauce on high for 1 minute and pour some of it over the chicken. Pass the remaining sauce separately.

Veal and Pasta Loaf with Tomato-Basil Ketchup

Serves 12
as a starter

Working time:
about 1 hour
and 10
minutes

Total time:
about 2 hours
and 20
minutes

Calories
143

Protein
6g

Cholesterol
55mg

Total fat
3g

Saturated fat
1g

Sodium
115 mg

500 g	veal topside or top rump, trimmed and minced	**1 lb**	**1**	egg white	**1**
1 tsp	olive oil	**1 tsp**	**250 g**	rigatoni	**8 oz**
1	onion, chopped	**1**	**1 tbsp**	cornflour	**1 tbsp**
1	small garlic clove, crushed	**1**	**15 cl**	semi-skimmed milk	**$\frac{1}{4}$ pint**
150 g	courgettes, trimmed and grated	**5 oz**	**$\frac{1}{4}$ tsp**	grated nutmeg	**$\frac{1}{4}$ tsp**
150 g	carrot, grated	**5 oz**	**1 tbsp**	freshly grated Parmesan Cheese	**1 tbsp**
150 g	parsnip, grated	**5 oz**		**Tomato-basil ketchup**	
$\frac{1}{2}$ tsp	salt	**$\frac{1}{2}$ tsp**	**750 g**	tomatoes, skinned and chopped	**1$\frac{1}{2}$ lb**
	freshly ground black pepper		**1 tsp**	tomato paste	**1 tsp**
1	egg	**1**	**$\frac{1}{2}$ tsp**	caster sugar	**$\frac{1}{2}$ tsp**
			6	fresh basil leaves, shredded	**6**

Gently heat the oil in a small frying pan and cook the onion, garlic and 2 tablespoons of water for about 5 minutes or until softened. Mix the onion and garlic in a bowl with the veal, courgettes, carrot, parsnip, half the salt and some pepper.

Lightly beat the egg and egg white together in a bowl. Add half to the veal mixture and mix well. Set aside. Cook the rigatoni in salted water until it is *al dente*.

For the white sauce, mix the cornflour with a little of the milk. Heat the remaining milk, add the cornflour mixture, and simmer gently for 3 minutes, stirring constantly. Remove from the heat and stir in the remaining egg mixture, salt and the nutmeg. Drain the pasta, put it back in the pan and mix with the white sauce

Preheat the oven to 170°C (325°F or Mark 3). Line the bottom of a loaf tin with greaseproof paper. Make a layer of one third of the meat mixture on the bottom of the tin. Cover with equal layers of pasta and meat mixture.

Prawn Teriyaki

Serves 4

Working time:
about 20
minutes

Total time:
about 30
minutes

Calories
125
Protein
17g
Cholesterol
130mg
Total fat
1g
Saturated fat
0g
Sodium
405mg

500 g	large raw prawns, peeled and deveined	**1 lb**
4 tbsp	sweet sherry	**4 tbsp**
2 tbsp	low-sodium soy sauce or shoyu	**2 tbsp**
1 tsp	rice vinegar	**1 tsp**
1	garlic clove, finely chopped	**1**
1	slice wholemeal bread	**1**

1 tsp	cornflour	**1 tsp**
12.5 cl	fish stock or dry white wine	**4 fl oz**
1	carrot peeled and julienned	**1**
3	spring onions, trimmed and cut into 5 cm (2 inch) pieces, the pieces thinly sliced lengthwise	**3**

Combine the sherry, soy sauce, vinegar and garlic in a bowl. Add the prawns and stir gently to coat them evenly. Marinate the prawns in the refrigerator for 20 minutes, stirring them from time to time.

Microwave the slice of bread on high for 2 minutes. Place the bread in a polythene bag and crush it into crumbs with a rolling pin.

Mix the cornflour with 1 tablespoon of the stock or wine. Strain the marinade into a glass bowl; stir in all but 2 tablespoons of the remaining stock or wine, along with the cornflour mixture. Microwave this sauce on high for 3 minutes. Stir the sauce until it is smooth, then set it aside.

Dip the prawns into the breadcrumbs to coat them on one side. Arrange the prawns, coated side up, in a shallow dish. Pour in the remaining stock or wine. Cover the dish and microwave it on high for 3 minutes. Rearrange the prawns, turning any uncooked pieces towards the edge of the dish.

Stir the carrot and spring onion strips into the sauce; pour the sauce around the prawns. Cover the dish again and cook it on medium high (70 per cent power) for 2 minutes. Allow the prawns to stand, covered, for another 2 minutes before transferring them to a serving dish. Spoon the sauce and vegetables around the prawns and serve immediately.

Granary Pizza with Sweetcorn and Pineapple

Serves 4

Working time:
about 40
minutes

Total time:
about 1 hour
and 45
minutes

Calories
395
Protein
17g
Cholesterol
15mg
Total fat
8g
Saturated fat
4g
Sodium
390mg

2 tbsp	grainy mustard	**2 tbsp**
350 g	sweetcorn kernels, cut from two large ears	**12 oz**
½ tsp	safflower oil	**½ tsp**
1	large onion, sliced into rings	**1**
4	black olives, stoned and quartered	**4**
2 tsp	chopped fresh basil, plus shredded basil leaves, for garnish	**2 tsp**
⅛ tsp	paprika	**⅛ tsp**
½	small ripe pineapple, skinned, cored and diced	**½**
1	red pepper, seeded, diced	**1**
90 g	Gouda cheese, grated	**3 oz**
	Pizza Dough	
125 g	granary flour	**4 oz**
125 g	plain flour	**4 oz**
½ tsp	salt	**½ tsp**
30 g	fresh yeast	**1 oz**

For the dough, mix both types of flour in a bowl with the salt. In a small bowl, crumble the fresh yeast over 15 cl (¼ pint) of warm water. Leave the mixture in a warm place for 10 minutes, until its surface has become frothy. Make a well in the centre of the dry ingredients and pour in the yeast. Mix the ingredients to a soft dough and knead for 5 minutes. Return the dough to the bowl, cover it, and leave in a warm place to rise.

Knock back the dough, then roll it out on a floured surface into a circle about 30 cm (12 inches) in diameter. Place on a baking sheet or pizza pan and brush with the mustard, leaving a border. Cover and leave to rise again.

Preheat the oven to 200°C (400°F or Mark 6). Cook the sweetcorn in a pan of simmering water for 3 minutes. Fry the onion rings for 5 to 6 minutes, until soft. Stir in the basil.

Arrange the onion and basil over the pizza base and sprinkle with the paprika. Scatter on the sweetcorn, pineapple, add the sweet pepper and olives and finally the cheese.

Bake the pizza in the oven for 20 to 25 minutes, until it is crusty round the edges and the cheese has melted. Serve hot.

Risotto with Carrots and Coriander

Serves 6

Working (and total) time: about 1 hour

Calories 300

Protein 5g

Cholesterol 30mg

Total fat 11 g

Saturated fat 6g

Sodium 155mg

45 g	unsalted butter	**1½ oz**
1	onion, finely chopped	**1**
1 litre	unsalted chicken stock	**1¼ pints**
2 tsp	ground coriander	**2 tsp**
300 g	carrots, peeled and finely diced	**10 oz**
350 g	Italian round -grain rice	**12 oz**

	freshly ground black pepper	
45 g	Parmesan cheese,	**1½ oz**
	freshly grated	
1	small bunch fresh	**1**
	coriander leaves, finely chopped	

In a large, heavy-bottomed pan, heat 30 g (1 oz) of the butter, and sauté the onion until it is transparent—3 to 5 minutes. Meanwhile, bring the stock to the boil in a saucepan, stir in the ground coriander, reduce the heat and keep the liquid simmering gently.

Add the diced carrots to the onion, and saute them for about 5 minutes. Add the rice, and stir well to ensure that the grains are coated with butter.

Ladle a few spoonfuls of the hot chicken stock into the rice, stir well, and let the mixture cook, stirring occasionally, until most of the liquid has been absorbed by the rice

Continue adding hot stock, a little at a time, stirring the mixture constantly and replenishing the liquid as the rice absorbs it. Cook the rice until it is moist but not swimming in the stock, and the grains have lost their brittleness but still retain a chewy core—about 20 minutes.

Remove the rice from the heat and add the remaining butter, the Parmesan cheese and some pepper. Stir the mixture well, cover the pan, and let the risotto stand for 5 minutes. Stir the rice once more, and sprinkle it with the coriander before serving.

Pork Kofta

Serves 4

Working time: about 35 minutes

Total time: about 2 hours and 30 minutes

Calories
375
Protein
30g
Cholesterol
80mg
Total fat
20g
Saturated fat
5g
Sodium
510mg

500 g	minced pork fillet	**1 lb**
1	lemon, grated rind only	**1**
2	garlic cloves, crushed	**2**
1 tbsp	coriander seeds, toasted and coarsely ground	**1 tbsp**
½ tsp	salt	**½ tsp**
	freshly ground black pepper	
3 tbsp	dry white wine	**3 tbsp**
1½ tbsp	fresh lemon juice	**1½ tbsp**
1½ tbsp	virgin olive oil	**1½ tbsp**
4	carrots, grated	**4**
30 g	fresh coriander leaves, chopped	**1 oz**
4	pitta breads	**4**

Combine the pork with the lemon rind, garlic, coriander seeds, salt and some pepper. Divide into four and roll into sausage shapes about 15 by 2.5 cm (6 by 1 inch). Gently place the kofta in a shallow dish and pour on the wine, 1 tablespoon of the lemon juice and the oil. Leave to marinate for at least 2 hours, turning the kofta and coating with the marinade at frequent intervals.

Preheat the grill to high. Mix the carrots with the coriander leaves and the remaining lemon juice.

Remove the kofta ·from the marinade and grill them until the pork is well browned—about 7 minutes. Meanwhile, warm the pitta bread in a 170°C (325°F or Mark 3) oven.

When the kofta are cooked, carefully slit open one side of each pitta bread to make a pocket. Fill with a quarter of the carrot salad and one hot kofta.

Chunky Beef Chili

Serves 8

Working time:
about 1 hour

Total time:
about 4 hours

Calories
230
Protein
27g
Cholesterol
75mg
Total fat
10g
Saturated fat
3g
Sodium
460mg

2	dried chili peppers, quartered	2	1 tbsp	dried oregano	1 tbsp
2	fresh green chili peppers, chopped	2	$\frac{1}{4}$ tsp	cayenne pepper	$\frac{1}{4}$ tsp
2 tbsp	safflower oil	2 tbsp	$\frac{1}{4}$ tsp	freshly ground black pepper	$\frac{1}{4}$ tsp
1 kg	braising steak, cut into chunks	2 lb	1 tbsp	plain flour	1 tbsp
2	large onions, finely chopped	2	400 g	canned tomatoes, coarsely chopped with their juice	14 oz
2	sticks celery, finely chopped	2			
2	garlic cloves, finely chopped	2	1	bay leaf	1
2 tbsp	fresh ginger root, chopped	2 tbsp	$1\frac{1}{2}$ tsp	salt	$1\frac{1}{2}$ tsp
1 tbsp	ground cumin	1 tbsp	$\frac{1}{2}$ tsp	grated orange rind	$\frac{1}{2}$ tsp

Put the dried chilies into a saucepan; pour in the litre (16 fl oz) of water and boil for 5 minutes. Let the chilies soften for 5 minutes then put them in a blender with 12.5 cl (4 fl oz) of their soaking liquid; reserve the remaining liquid. Add the fresh chili peppers and purée until very smooth then strain through a sieve into the reserved soaking liquid.

Heat $\frac{1}{2}$ tablespoon of the oil in a heavy frying pan over medium-high heat. Add about one quarter of the beef chunks and cook, turning frequently, until they are well browned—approximately 8 minutes. Transfer

to a heavy pan. Brown the rest of the meat.

Add the $\frac{1}{2}$ tablespoon of oil to the frying pan along with the onions, celery and garlic. Sauté for 5 minutes, stirring frequently. Stir in the ginger, cumin, oregano, cayenne pepper and black pepper, and cook for 1 minute. Add the flour and cook for 1 minute more, stirring constantly. Transfer to the pan.

Pour the reserved chili mixture and $\frac{1}{2}$ litre (16 fl oz) of water into the pan. Stir in the tomatoes and their juice along with the bay leaf, salt and orange rind. Gently cook until the meat is tender—$2\frac{1}{2}$ to 3 hours.

Useful weights and measures

Weight Equivalents

Avoirdupois		*Metric*
1 ounce	=	28.35 grams
1 pound	=	254.6 grams
2.3 pounds	=	1 kilogram

Liquid Measurements

$^1/_4$ pint	=	$1^1/_2$ decilitres
$^1/_2$ pint	=	$^1/_4$ litre
scant 1 pint	=	$^1/_2$ litre
$1^3/_4$ pints	=	1 litre
1 gallon	=	4.5 litres

Liquid Measures

1 pint	= 20 fl oz	= 32 tablespoons
$^1/_2$ pint	= 10 fl oz	= 16 tablespoons
$^1/_4$ pint	= 5 fl oz	= 8 tablespoons
$^1/_8$ pint	= $2^1/_2$ fl oz	= 4 tablespoons
$^1/_{16}$ pint	= $1^1/_4$ fl oz	= 2 tablespoons

Solid Measures

1 oz almonds, ground = $3^3/_4$ level tablespoons
1 oz breadcrumbs fresh = 7 level tablespoons
1 oz butter, lard = 2 level tablespoons
1 oz cheese, grated = $3^1/_2$ level tablespoons
1 oz cocoa = $2^3/_4$ level tablespoons
1 oz desiccated coconut = $4^1/_2$ tablespoons
1 oz cornflour = $2^1/_2$ tablespoons
1 oz custard powder = $2^1/_2$ tablespoons
1 oz curry powder and spices = 5 tablespoons
1 oz flour = 2 level tablespoons
1 oz rice, uncooked = $1^1/_2$ tablespoons
1 oz sugar, caster and granulated = 2 tablespoons
1 oz icing sugar = $2^1/_2$ tablespoons
1 oz yeast, granulated = 1 level tablespoon

American Measures

16 fl oz	=1 American pint
8 fl oz	=1 American standard cup
0.50 fl oz	=1 American tablespoon

(slightly smaller than British Standards Institute tablespoon)

0.16 fl oz	=1 American teaspoon

Australian Cup Measures
(Using the 8-liquid-ounce cup measure)

1 cup flour	4 oz
1 cup sugar (crystal or caster)	8 oz
1 cup icing sugar (free from lumps)	5 oz
1 cup shortening (butter, margarine)	8 oz
1 cup brown sugar (lightly packed)	4 oz
1 cup soft breadcrumbs	2 oz
1 cup dry breadcrumbs	3 oz
1 cup rice (uncooked)	6 oz
1 cup rice (cooked)	5 oz
1 cup mixed fruit	4 oz
1 cup grated cheese	4 oz
1 cup nuts (chopped)	4 oz
1 cup coconut	$2^1/_2$ oz

Australian Spoon Measures

	level tablespoon
1 oz flour	2
1 oz sugar	$1^1/_2$
1 oz icing sugar	2
1 oz shortening	1
1 oz honey	1
1 oz gelatine	2
1 oz cocoa	3
1 oz cornflour	$2^1/_2$
1 oz custard powder	$2^1/_2$

Australian Liquid Measures
(Using 8-liquid-ounce cup)

1 cup liquid	8 oz
$2^1/_2$ cups liquid	20 oz (1 pint)
2 tablespoons liquid	1 oz
1 gill liquid	5 oz ($^1/_4$ pint)